HOW TO MOTIVATE MEN

HOW TO MOTIVATE MEN

Jack H. McQuaig

FREDERICK FELL INC.

NEW YORK

New Printing, 1973

For information address:
Frederick Fell, Inc.
386 Park Avenue South
New York, N. Y. 10016

Library of Congress Catalog Card No. 67-12667

Published simultaneously in Canada by
George J. McLeod, Limited, Toronto 2B, Ontario

Manufactured in the United States of America

TO PETER, DON AND JOHN

CONTENTS

HOW TO MOTIVATE MEN

INTRODUCTION

We all look with awe on the great administrators and top executives in gigantic corporations. These men have the capacity to move from one business to another, and with their magic touch take organizations that are losing money and turn them into profitable operations.

They help an electrical appliance business out of trouble and then move to a steel corporation that needs help, then on to head up a department store or an insurance company that is floundering. In each case, they are able to pull that organization back from the brink of failure and build it into a successful enterprise. How do they do it?

That's what you want to know. How do they do it and can you get to do it in the same way?

Before we answer these questions, let's take a look at the reasons why these great executives are successful. On close examination of their performance, we must admit that their success is mostly due to their ability to motivate men and get results through people.

In the junior jobs in any organization, the technical skills are most important. To succeed at the lower levels a man must be technically competent at his trade. If he is an accountant, his success will be due to his knowledge and skill in accounting. If he is a lathe operator, his success will be due to his knowledge and skill as a lathe operator. If he is a salesman, his success will be due to his knowledge and skill as a salesman. However, as he moves up to the supervisory level, he no longer does the technical work himself, but he must get other people to do it for him. In this new job, he must learn a complete new set of skills: the skills of supervising and motivating people.

Top executives frankly admit that they know little

about the businesses that they rehabilitate. It would be impossible for them to have complete technical knowledge of the various firms they revamp from failure to success. Of course, they do gain a general knowledge of each business as they work in it, but this knowledge is only superficial. For real know-how, they are dependent on the technically trained executives in each corporation.

The secret of success of these great men, then, is not in knowing how to do it themselves, but in gaining the cooperation of those who do have the know-how. To do this, they must be experts in the art of developing men, motivating them, and supervising their work.

You too can become skilled in this art of motivating others. In this book, I will attempt to show you how the great masters succeed. If you can put these techniques and principles to work, you too will have outstanding success. You will learn how to go into a department, a division, or an organization and by delegating work to men, gaining their confidence, (and motivating them) you will be able to achieve success.

The same techniques and principles of delegating, leading, and motivating others apply in all areas of a business; in all departments large or small; or in a situation where you are directing the efforts of only one person, such as a secretary or an executive assistant. These same principles apply at every level. The front-line supervisor uses the same basic methods of motivating and dealing with men as the top executive.

Through research and study, techniques have been developed for working with men which we might label as "Principles of Supervision or Man Management."

These principles of supervision and the skills in applying them are the keys to success at every level of supervision and management in business. The higher up you go in your job the more you will depend on your skills of managing and motivating men. If you arrive at the president's job, you will find very little of your time is spent with technical problems. Mostly you will be working on problems of human relations, public relations, labor relations, planning, organizing, controlling, and developing people. Nearly all these problems require skill in motivating men.

1

THE IMPORTANCE OF SOUND
TECHNIQUES OF MOTIVATION

Unfortunately, in the field of dealing with people, we do not have any definite laws or rules. We only have principles. In the physical sciences, we do have definite laws and rules. We know, for example, that water freezes at a certain temperature. We know that if we drop anything, it falls to the ground at a certain definite speed. This is known as the law of gravity. However, when we deal with men in a specific way, we cannot exactly predict how they will react.

Suppose, for example, in your job, you were to become so frustrated with one particular man that you were to strike him. What would he do? There is no definite law or rule to predict his behavior, is there? He might, for example, do these things: If he was a very religious person, he might turn the other cheek. If he was a fearful, cowardly person, he might slink away and say nothing. If he was a typical red-blooded man, he might up and strike you back. If he was an ex-prizefighter, he might proceed to beat you up. If he was a psychopathic killer, he might pick up the nearest blunt instrument and beat you to death.

What happens when you strike a man or when you do anything with a man depends on many things about him as an individual. His behavior will be influenced considerably by his background, his training, his attitudes, his philosophy of life, his education, his prejudices, his temperament, and his emotional make-up. Therefore, the more we know about the individual men who are working for us, the better understanding we will have of them and the better job we will do in motivating them.

For this reason, the ability to appraise men and understand them is one of the most important skills for any supervisor to master.

In addition to the particular knowledge of the individual which helps us in guiding and managing him, we also have certain general principles of human behavior which act as guides.

Regardless of whether you work in production, accounting, sales, engineering, advertising, personnel, or purchasing, you will have one problem in common with all supervisors. That problem is People. People are difficult. They have their strengths and weaknesses, their ups and downs, their joys and sorrows, and you don't have to be supervising men for long before you find out two things about them.

First, you find that it is very difficult to change people. Those of you who have ever tried to make a lazy man work know what I mean. Those of you who have ever tried to make an inflexible person get along with others know what I mean. The second thing you learn is that men don't like being bossed by other men. Some men are so inflexible that unless they originate an idea themselves, they are incapable of carrying it out.

This makes your job as a supervisor very difficult. How tough can they make it for you? Here they say as a supervisor you must delegate. Don't do it yourself. Get other people to do it for you. Don't do anything yourself that you can train or develop others to do. Keep your time free to organize, plan, and develop people. This is a sound philosophy. But then they give you difficult people to work with. They give you people you can't change and people who won't do what you tell them.

This job of motivating others is just about as tough as any job you could tackle. What is the answer? How can you be effective as a motivator of men?

There is one thing you can do. You can understand men. If you understand them, you can guide them, you can counsel them, you can lead them. Men are hungry for leadership, but it must be leadership that understands them and sees their point of view. Such leadership can rouse the spirit of men. It can make men do things that they are almost incapable of doing.

Are you a good leader? Answer this question and I will give you the answer. Are you working for your men or are they working for you? If your men are working for you, I will say that you may run a good department. You may have satisfactory performance and things may be going reasonably well. However, if you are working for your men, you are probably operating an outstanding department with production right at the top, and your boss is looking around for more supervisors like you.

Your job as a supervisor is to work for your men, to bring them the training, the supervision and the guidance they need to do an outstanding job. And to provide them with a climate and a set of working conditions in which they can work and satisfy their needs.

It's like this: When a man is born, he has need of clothing, food, water, shelter, rest, change, warmth, love, etc. These are the basic needs. Life becomes a struggle for each person to satisfy these needs. This is why money is important, because money will buy most of these basic needs, such as food, clothing, a house. Money is a very important motivator especially when you give extra money for extra effort.

As each person grows up, he develops the need to feel

important, to be well liked, to help others, etc. These are psychological needs. Although money helps to buy certain psychological needs, many of these needs cannot be bought. What satisfies these psychological needs is the way you treat a man on the job and the environment in which he works. The most successful executives know how to establish a set of working conditions on the job which will satisfy the psychological needs of their men.

These needs are just as important as the basic needs, and the supervisor who fails to recognize this is usually a failure at his job.

Psychological needs are as follows:

SECURITY—the feeling that he is liked and understood.

RECOGNITION—being appreciated, made to feel important, and given credit for his good work.

SENSE OF BELONGING—being needed and feeling that he is helping to achieve the goals of the company.

BEING TREATED WITH RESPECT AND DIGNITY— men want to feel that they are respected.

OPPORTUNITY—the possibility of improving himself and developing while he is on the job.

SATISFACTION FROM ACHIEVEMENT—having a job which he is capable of doing and which he gets a thrill out of doing well, a job which is a challenge to him and his skills and ability.

PURPOSE—the feeling that he is contributing to a worthwhile cause.

COMPETITION—a challenge and an opportunity for healthy competition with others in the organization will make him more interested in the job.

These are the psychological needs which men must satisfy on the job. The successful manager of men is the man who can provide a climate and a set of conditions in which men may satisfy these needs while they work on the job to satisfy the needs of the supervisor for efficiency and increased production.

Some executives are scornful of the psychological needs. They feel that only money counts and that if you want to motivate men, you must pay them more money. Most experienced supervisors realize that money is a motivating factor to a certain point only and that men will not work for money if they don't get recognition, respect, and opportunity to develop themselves.

The successful supervisor uses techniques to develop his men which will help them to satisfy the psychological as well as the basic needs. For example, he counsels his men and coaches them. He may rotate them in their jobs to give them more experience. At regular intervals, he appraises their work to let them know how they are doing and where they can improve themselves. He constructively criticizes their work in such a way that they like it and feel it is a form of recognition. He commends them for good work and gives them full credit for new ideas. He keeps training and guiding them constantly to help them achieve their greatest potential on the job.

Men appreciate the supervisor's effort to help them, and they cooperate and work for him to give him the maximum production.

I propose to show you how the successful manager performs all the functions of his job in such a way that he satisfies both the basic and psychological needs of his men. For example, take one of the basic functions of supervision: the giving of orders. There is a right way and a wrong way to give an order. As a supervisor, you may order a man to do a job without consideration for his need for security, recognition, a sense of belonging, satisfaction from achievement, opportunity for advancement, being treated with dignity as an individual and a sense of purpose in his work. On the other hand, it is possible for you to give orders in such a way as to recognize all these needs in the man and enable him to satisfy these needs while he is carrying out the order.

In each chapter, I will take one of the basic tasks of the supervisor, such as counseling, reprimanding, coaching, disciplining, training, appraising, delegating, and reviewing performance, and illustrate how you, as a supervisor, can perform it as the great masters of administration do: in such a way as to satisfy the needs of your men, which motivates them to work harder and develop themselves to do a better job for you.

2

MOTIVATION OR MANIPULATION?

One thing we all discover very early in life is that people don't like being pushed around or bossed by others. People don't like being told to do things. People don't like being supervised. Some people don't even like being asked to do things.

Men get this resistance to supervision or bossing from their early experiences in life. As soon as a new-born baby is old enough to start reaching for things or walking over things, his parents are shouting at him, "Don't do that"; "Stop doing this"; "Watch out for that."

From the very first efforts and movements we make on our own, we have some boss or supervisor trying to restrain us. No wonder we all resent supervision. It's surprising that we can tolerate it under any circumstances. Some of us can't tolerate it.

Because some parents are exceptionally strict and overly protective with children, they arouse in the child a resentment of all attempts to control him. If this parental control is unfair or excessively strict or cruel, it builds up a resentment in the child against human interference of any kind. A child raised by parents of this type will grow up subconsciously resenting authority and resisting it. Sometimes he will automatically go against every attempt of others to direct him. He develops a habit of resisting authority which will stick with him the rest of his life. Not only will he resent unfair discipline, but he will also resist fair discipline. He is the person who is described as being "uncooperative" or "inflexible."

The early restrictions and the early discipline we experience as children often sets our attitude toward supervision. Naturally, all children have to be controlled even in the very early days because the very young child is completely free of any self-regulation. He will spill things and break valuable articles and sometimes hurt himself seriously unless some restriction is placed on his behavior.

Some parents can guide the young child with a minimum of direct resistance, and by a loving form of control and direction, can spare the child the feelings of frustration which come from direct orders and strong head-on resistance. Men who are raised by parents who are more subtle in their discipline are likely to adjust more easily to supervision.

Nobody likes close supervision, but some people can adjust to it easier than others.

Equally important in determining a man's attitudes and reactions to supervision are the characteristics which he inherits from his parents. Some men are born with a temperament which drives them to supervise others and causes them to be resistant to supervision. Other men are born with a temperament which causes them to be more submissive and to accept supervision more readily. So men start out in life with a great variation in their tolerance of supervision.

The strongest supervisors are those men who do not really supervise people but who lead them. In fact, the best leaders lean over backwards to avoid any bossing or dominating of employees. They try to sell men on working and they provide working conditions which will cause their men to want to work. They try indirectly to get men to want to do a good job.

The ideal boss is one who does not make his men feel that they are working for him, but rather that he is working for them. He is working to bring them the best in training, guidance, working conditions, etc. In return, his men go to work to achieve what he wants: more production and efficiency.

The key to getting men to work is to get them to want to achieve something. The human mind and emotions are so constituted that the only way we can get real cooperation and effort from men is to get them to want to do something.

The question which supervisors ask themselves more frequently than any other is: HOW DO I MOTIVATE MEN? How do I get them to work? If you had the answer to this problem, you would have the answer to good supervision. This is what the supervisor is paid to do. This is what management expects him to do. He must get men to cooperate and collaborate and work as a team to achieve the goals of management.

Unfortunately, many supervisors without training, without knowledge of people, try to push men and force them to work. It seems like the easy way, the quick way, the short way. To give orders and be demanding and push people around requires no thought or effort. Unfortunately, this method doesn't work well because of the built-in resistance people have to being bossed.

Suppose we take the job of supervision right from the very beginning and see what is going on in the mind of both the supervisor and the man who is going to work for him. Let's assume that you have a man in front of you who is applying for a position and who plans to work under your direction. What is he thinking? He may not be aware of it consciously, but in his subconscious mind, here are his thoughts:

"Mr. Supervisor, I know what you want from me on this job. You want me to be loyal. You want me to work hard. You want me to be thorough. You want me to co-operate with others and work well as part of a team. You want me to be creative. You want me to be punctual. The things which you would like in me as an employee are obvious. I am well aware of all these things, and believe me, I can deliver this kind of performance. In fact, it is just as easy for me to work this way as it is for me to be a goldbricker, a leadswinger, or a fellow who does it the easy way. It is more satisfying to me when I am productive and doing a good job.

"However, Mr. Supervisor, have you considered that I have certain basic things that I want from the job? I'll make a deal with you. If you give me the things I want, I'll give you the things you want. There's only one catch in this proposition, Mr. Supervisor: I don't think you really know what I want. So how can you give me what I want if you don't even know what it is?

"Now if you will sit down here and listen to me, I'll tell you all the things I want from this job, and then you tell me if you can give them to me. If you can promise me these conditions, you will have on your staff one of the most dedicated men you have ever seen. I will give you all the productive effort, all the hard work, all the thoroughness, all the loyalty, all the creativity, all the capacity to work as part of a team that you could desire. In other words, I will stretch myself to give everything possible to the job if you will in return give me the things I need. Is that a fair deal? All right, here goes.

"The first thing I want from this job is security. By this, you think I mean pension plans, guaranteed wages, medical benefits and extra pay for extra effort. How right you are. I do want all of these things. These financial benefits are very important to me because I have a wife and family at home and you could never pay me enough to satisfy all their needs. However, Mr. Supervisor, have you ever thought that security means something more than this to me, something that maybe you haven't considered to be important?

"It means a friendly atmosphere in which to work. This is important because it makes me feel that I am accepted by you and liked by you. Just as important to this feeling of security is knowing that you, as my individual boss, understand me; that you are trying to help me; that you are working with me to develop and improve my skills.

"Anything you can do to show an interest in my life off the job is helpful. Not a prying or spying interest in my personal affairs, but rather an awareness that I have a family and other interests beyond the job. It is important to me to know that you are interested in me as an individual person, not just in what you can squeeze out of me on the job.

"To me it is important that I can approach you with problems, that you are friendly, and that I can talk things over with you. This is very helpful to my basic security. Other things that matter are that you treat me fairly and let me know where I stand at all times; when you make a promise to me, live up to it. If I make an error or if I have had some misunderstanding, I would like to feel that you, as my boss, will stand behind me.

"Mr. Supervisor, to sum this all up one of the most important things in the world to me is to have the feeling that you, as my immediate boss, like me as a person, understand me and will try to help me. Why is this important? Because you are one of the most important persons in the world to me. I know that if you like me and understand me, you will try to help me and develop me to do the things of which I am capable.

"On the other hand, I know that if you dislike me, it won't matter how hard I work; how much experience

I have; how much education or training I have, or what I contribute to the job, you can cut me down to any size you want. You have a tremendous power over me as an individual, and therefore, the feeling that you like me is a very basic part of my security.

"The second thing I would like on the job, Mr. Supervisor, is recognition. By this you think I want credit for any new ideas that I discover. You think that I want everybody to know about it if I think of something new on the job. You also think that I want my picture on the front page of the company magazine from time to time, that I want to be in the spotlight. You are right about this. I do want this kind of recognition. However, recognition means something more to me.

"I would like to feel that you, as my immediate boss, occasionally recognize my good work. The fact that you take time out to tell me when I do a job well is very important. You can show this recognition in many ways. You can give me recognition by listening to me when I have a grievance or a complaint. If I give you a suggestion, the fact that you will consider this suggestion and try to make it work is important. If it won't work, it will be helpful to know why. Another subtle form of recognition is the fact that when you assign some work to me, you leave me on my own. This shows that you have confidence in me. Occasionally, it helps if you will take time out to criticize me constructively. Not the kind of criticism that cuts me down to size, but the kind that builds me up. I like the kind of constructive criticism that makes me feel you are trying to help me do a better job, that you are trying to develop and guide me.

"The best kind of recognition, of course, is direct praise for a job well done. Asking my opinion and asking my advice on problems also gives me an indirect form of recognition. How about taking me in behind the scenes, where possible, and telling me the "why" behind things. This makes me feel that I am an important member of the team.

"Another very important thing to me is the feeling of belonging. This is rather difficult to explain, but it is something like this: I like to feel that I am useful. This makes me feel secure. I like to feel that the people around me accept me and think that I am an asset to the team. I like to feel that I am a part of something bigger than myself, and I want to be liked and accepted by people on the job. You can help me a lot in this by helping others to accept me.

"You can also give me this feeling of belonging by taking me into your confidence occasionally. Any time you can tell me things about company policy, I will get the feeling that I am part of the team. Tell me what is going on behind the scenes. If you ask my opinions and listen to my suggestions, these are indications that you don't underrate me, and that you feel I am worthwhile.

"Maybe I can sum up this feeling of belonging best by making a very extreme statement. The ideal in belonging would be that I was such an important part of this organization that if anything were to happen to me, the whole company would fall apart. Knowing that you just can't operate without me gives me that feeling of belonging to the greatest degree.

"A feeling of self-respect is also vital. You can help me to achieve this by providing the right climate on the job. The feeling that you have respect for my dignity as an individual person and accept me as an equal is important. These things help me to have self-respect. It boils down to very simple things. Don't criticize me openly in front of others, or threaten me. Give me responsibility and reasonable freedom in carrying out my duties. Trust me and don't supervise me so closely that I can't use my initiative.

"Opportunity for advancement is something else which

I need on the job. Oh, I know what you think. You think that I would like to someday become vice president of the company. You are right. I would like to be a vice president. Everybody wants a title and status. However, I realize that there are a limited number of jobs at the top and maybe I am not capable of going to the top. However, always give me the opportunity to keep improving.

"It is important to me that I make progress. As long as I am with you, I would like to feel that I am improving myself so that when I leave I will be a better man than when I came to work with you. You can give me this feeling of progress in many ways; give me varied experiences by alternating me on different jobs, so I can learn other skills; send me on training courses and seminars outside the company; give me training on the job.

"Something else, of course, that is vital to me is satisfaction from achievement. This is just simply, Mr. Boss, that I would like a job that I am capable of doing. One that is not too difficult for me, and yet not beyond my capacity. And give me the training and coaching to do it well. It is fun to do anything well. It is my responsibility to work hard to master the job, but it is your responsibility to place me in the right job and to give me the guidance that will enable me to master it.

"This is the greatest motivator of all, as you know. If you can put me into a situation where I get a thrill out of doing the job because I've mastered it, you will get me working at a pace that will be unbelievable to you.

"You can also make me feel that there is a purpose in my job by spelling out the goals of the company and by showing me how I help to achieve those goals. I don't just mean the purpose in dollars and profits, I mean the big purpose. What service does the company contribute to the community? I can catch fire for a purpose that is worth while and I am more likely to work for a purpose that is helping others than just to make big profits.

"How about competition? Anything you can do, Mr. Supervisor, to set up a situation in the company whereby I can feel that I'm part of a team competing with others will help. Anything that takes the job out of the routine and puts it into the nature of a game will stimulate my interest in the work I am doing and will make the job a little more enjoyable. Competition gives me something to strive for. Goals that I have a voice in setting, that give me something definite to aim at with my fellow workers, put some fun into the job, and I find this stimulating.

"Money? I am leaving this to the last. Not because it is the least important. It gives me the basic security of food, housing, and clothing. Extra money to put in the bank will make me feel that I have security when things get tough and times are not as good as they are today. Money will also help me to buy certain forms of recognition and opportunity.

"Extra money for extra effort is vital, but don't feel that it is the only important thing. You could double or quadruple my salary and still if you failed to respect me, and took away the things that satisfy my psychological needs, I would quit and go to work for somebody else. No strong man will work in a situation where he fails to get respect."

As a supervisor, you may say, "This is too complicated for me. I haven't got time to worry about all these fancy needs that people have. I've got a business to run. I have production to get out. My job is to get sales, produce the product or keep efficient accounting records. I haven't got time to pamper people, hold hands with them or have them crying on my shoulder. This isn't an old ladies' home or a women's missionary society. Can't you give me something simpler than this? Can't you give me some easy way to motivate people? I must have an easier way because I haven't time for this fancy work which you describe."

The answer to these questions, of course, is Yes. I can give you a very simple way, a very easy way to motivate men. The advantage of this easy way is that it requires no thought. It doesn't require any intelligence. Anybody can do it. It works quickly and it usually gets results in a hurry. What is it?

When you want a man to work, threaten him and criticize him openly. Threaten to fire him. This is the way the bull of the woods used to do it. When he threatened to fire a man, that man would respond because he was afraid of losing his job. The problem with this technique is that after you put on the pressure and get the work out, you haven't done anything to change the man. When the pressure is taken off, he will relax back to the same old attitudes that he had before. The next time you want him to work, you will have to put more pressure on him. After a while the pressure gets to have less and less effect and you have to use bigger threats and a bigger needle.

Another weakness in this technique is that it usually turns a man against you. When he sees that you are not interested in his welfare, he soon loses interest in your welfare. If he resents the way you are using him, he will show this resentment by deliberately slowing down his work or by doing sloppy work or staying away from the job or deliberately breaking the machinery.

This technique of getting people to work is called manipulation. It is called manipulation because by this method the supervisor is getting his men to do the things he wants done, without any thought for their interests. What he is really saying to his men is, "Here's what I want you to do; now go out and do it because I say so or because I want it done. I don't care about your interests;

all I'm concerned about is what I want: more productivity and more efficiency. If you don't give me that, you're going to be in trouble. I'll fire you, demote you, lower your pay, etc."

The man who motivates people, on the other hand, is saying to them, "I have to get production out; I need efficiency. This is very important to me and to the company. However, I realize that you have needs too. You have needs for security, for recognition, belonging, etc. I'll make you a proposition. You give me the hard work I want, and I'll give you the opportunity to satisfy your needs on the job. I'll provide a climate and a set of working conditions in which you can satisfy all your needs while you're satisfying my need for productivity."

Analyze the difference between manipulation and motivation and you end up by saying this: "The manipulator doesn't get very good results from his people because he fails in the most important thing of all in human relations, he fails to get people to *want* to do the job. The only way we can ever motivate people is to get them to "want" to do something. Whenever a man wants to do something, not only will he go out and do what you are asking, but he will use his own intelligence to think up other ways of doing it better. So if you can get him to want to do it, you've got him motivated in a way that is sometimes almost unbelievable.

Slave labor, where you whip men to get them to work, is the most inefficient form of labor. When the whip is applied, men will work, but as soon as the man with the whip goes out of sight, they take it easy and drag their feet. In total productivity, slave labor is the most inefficient labor, because the supervisor, who is trying to motivate his men, fails to do the most important thing of all. He fails to make his men want to do the job.

So, Mr. Boss, give me the things I want, and I will

give you the things you want. Give me the things I want, and you will get me wanting to achieve the things you want, which are more production and more efficiency. These are the things that I know you need, and I will give them to you if you will give me the things I need.

3

THE IMPORTANCE OF APPRAISING MEN

As a supervisor, you have two kinds of knowledge to help you motivate people: the broad general knowledge of human relations which you have accumulated over the years from your experience in working with men and the detailed knowledge of the individuals on your staff.

The more you know about a man's early background, education, hobbies, social life, health, religion, work history, present family life, etc., the more you will understand him and the better job you will do of motivating him. This specific knowledge is also of great help in appraising men and revealing their strengths and weaknesses. It is absolutely necessary to have this knowledge of a man if you are to make wise decisions in hiring and promoting.

When you hire a new man, it is usually difficult to know how to work with him at the beginning because you have little real knowledge of him. As you get to know more about his background, training, family, hobbies, social interests, etc., you can do a better job of motivating him because you understand him. The more you know about him, the better you will be able to work with him.

It is important to any supervisor that he develop a technique for appraising the attitudes, temperament, and character of men. One of the most important things you do in your job is to hire a man. Your success as a supervisor depends on your ability to get results through people, not so much to achieve these results yourself, but to select and develop subordinates who can achieve them for you.

If you hire good men, you make your job easy. If you hire weak men, you make your job impossible. Good men, who have the ability to do their jobs well, cause you no trouble. If all your people were top quality, your job would be simple. Weak men, on the other hand, are a constant worry. Hire them and you take on permanent personnel problems and make your job very difficult.

Most supervisors spend thirty to seventy per cent of their time correcting, guiding, and motivating the problem people in their organizations. Therefore, if you could spot these problem people before you hired them, weed them out, and hire top producers instead, you could increase your output without increasing your effort. You could get more work done in the same time. And you could free yourself to make decisions, to plan and think creatively, to prepare yourself for the next step up the ladder.

For example, many organizations have found that twenty per cent of their salesmen sell eighty per cent of their output.

Try to imagine having all your salesmen like your best salesman, all your accountants like your best accountant, all your foremen like your best foreman, and all your production and clerical workers like your best workers.

Most top supervisors have learned early in their careers that it is almost impossible to size up men merely by looking at them or by chatting with them casually. These executives have learned that superficial appearances, personality, and a glib tongue are deceptive.

Most new supervisors, on the other hand, usually start by appraising men according to: their appearance, their ability to express themselves well, their sociability and personality.

In other words, they choose a subordinate because he looks and acts good or because they like him.

And then, months or years later, after many of these "good looking" men have been fired, the executives who hired them find that some of their most effective employees have the following attributes:

They are unimpressive in appearance—may perhaps be pale, skinny anaemic.

They may have little ability to express themselves. Their handshakes may be moist and limp. They may have little or no personality. These men are successful at their jobs not because of their appearance or personality, but because they have positive attitudes, strong drive, steady persistence, mature character, and marked aptitude for getting along with others.

These are the characteristics you are looking for. These are the inner traits that make a man a success. Let's look at them carefully.

1. *Positive attitudes*. The ability to say YES. To try. To expect success. To believe in himself and others.

2. *Strong drive*. Top capacity for work. The ability to break down barriers. Internal motivation.

3. *Steady persistence*. Determination. The will to never quit. To keep on trying when others give up.

4. *Mature character*. Reliability. Realistic thinking. The ability to take hard knocks. Good judgment. Self-control. The capacity to consider the interests of others.

5. *Aptitude for getting along with others*. Other aptitudes and skills. Good general intelligence.

Every one of these is an inner trait. None of them can be seen in a man's appearance or learned from a casual conversation. They are revealed only in action and over long periods of time. In your first meeting with a man, you have to dig for them. You have to uncover them, piece by piece.

You have to trace out their patterns from the life history of the man in front of you. And you can't do this by casual conversation. It can only be done by scientific questioning.

When you appraise a man, look deeper than his superficial qualities. Forget about personal appearance and charm. Judge him not by personality, but by character. Search for the inner traits, where the real man is hiding.

Contrary to popular opinion, most highly successful men are not leaders in their special field of work because they have an inborn aptitude for it. They are successful in that field because, from the very beginning, they worked hard at the job, mastered it, and came to like it. In other words, they became experts in their field and were motivated by the sheer thrill of accomplishment.

It was their character, and not their aptitude, that made them leaders in that field. Aptitude is often wasted. Character expresses itself irresistibly.

The sound appraisal of men is based on this theory: Men inherit much of their personality, temperament, and character, and much of it is shaped by the early days of their lives. After these childhood days, their basic character and personality changes little.

Therefore, choose your men on the basis of their history, rather than by hiring any man who comes along and then trying to change him to fit the needs of the job. If you need hard workers, choose men who have already proven themselves to be hard workers. If you want strong leaders, choose men who have already proven that they have leadership ability.

A man's character is already formed by the time you hire him. Make sure that character fits the requirements of the job from the day he starts to work, or both he and you will be in trouble.

This doesn't mean, of course, that people do not change as they mature. We all know that everybody changes slightly with every experience. Every time we read a book, every time we meet a new person, every time we face some adversity, this causes us to change slightly.

However, these are superficial changes. The real basic personality, temperament, and character of a man change very little.

Let me ask you to think back for a minute to some of the people that you have known well for a long time. Will you admit that those friends who are now hard-working, driving, dedicated, determined, ambitious have always been that way? If so, I will say to you that they will be that way ten years from now.

How about that easy-going, casual friend who is lacking in intensity and drive, who is carefree, happy-go-lucky, and enjoying life completely? Hasn't he always been that way? If so, he will be that way ten years from now.

And how about that difficult friend who can't get along with people? He has the knack of rubbing people the wrong way. He tends to involve himself in conflicts with others. Hasn't he always been that way? Of course, and ten years from now he will be the same.

Behavior patterns are deep-seated and, as such, form the basic personality. Down deep, people don't change, unless, perhaps, they face extreme adversity.

We all know of alcoholics who have changed themselves through Alcoholics Anonymous. Or men who find religion. Or men who change through extreme sickness. Or men who marry the right girl or the wrong girl. They sometimes come out of these experiences with a new way of looking at things, which changes their attitudes and behavior.

But these are the extremes. The normal person goes through life controlled by the character he inherited and formed during his childhood years. And it is this basic character we must look for. This basic fact—that men

change so little—makes it possible for us to develop a
scientific technique for appraising and understanding them.

This technique is simple.* By knowing what questions
to ask a man about his background and past experiences,
and by knowing how to interpret his answers, we can form
an estimate of what kind of a man he has been in the past.
In this way, we can draw a blueprint of his past pattern
of behavior habits. He leaves a trail as he goes through
life which reveals his attitudes, temperament, and character.

Once we have established this behavior pattern, we
can predict his probable future behavior because we know
he won't change fundamentally as he goes through life.

Let us sum it up:

If from questioning a man you can reconstruct the
situations he has been exposed to in the past, and if you
do it in such a way that you can get his attitudes toward
these situations and some information about his past behavior, you can just about tell the kind of person he has
been.

Then, once you know the kind of person he was in the
past, you can approximately predict the kind of person he
will be in the future.

When you become skilled in this simple technique,
you will be far more effective in hiring and promoting the
best men available, and in working effectively with them in
any kind of job. Remember, you can only be successful
with people insofar as you understand them and see their
point of view, which comes from knowing something about
their background.

For example, a young executive was offered a new job
soon after he mastered this simple technique of appraising
men. In his new position as manager of a small company,
he had about forty people on his staff. His first executive

* See *How To Pick Men* by Jack H. McQuaig, published
by Frederick Fell, Inc.

act was to sit down with each staff member for about an hour.

He attempted to find out everything that had happened to these people in the past. After he had completed this type of interviewing with the members of his new staff, he had almost as much insight into their characters as if he had known them for years. With this information at his fingertips, he was in a much stronger position to deal effectively with each employee.

What specific things do we want to know about a man in order to appraise his past performance? What are some of the direct questions we should ask him to get the information needed to appraise him?

Early Family Life

The first thing we want to know is something about his childhood life. In the early days, when he was forming his basic character, he lived with his family in an environment which molded and developed his personality and temperament.

Some psychiatrists say that a person's temperament and character are well formed by the age of four or five. However, we must admit that family influence on a person up to the age of eighteen or twenty can be critical.

This is confirmed by psychological research on juvenile delinquents and hardened criminals. This research has shown the overwhelming impact upon these men of broken homes or homes affected by divorce, alcoholism or family conflict. These factors may determine a man's entire future, causing him to live a constructive, positive life or to challenge the law and live completely for his own selfish interests.

If it is true that early family life has such a profound

influence on delinquents and criminals, it certainly must have a great effect on the normal person.

Specific facts that you should ask about concerning the early family life are these:

What kind of people were his father and mother?

How many brothers and sisters did he have, and what was their influence on him?

What was the economic level of the family?

Did money come easy in the early days or did he have to work for it and thereby develop good work habits?

Education

The next area you should examine is his educational background.

I have seen too many very capable presidents of large corporations who had only one or two years of high school education to be impressed with formal education as a criterion of business success.

On the other hand, we can learn a great deal about a man by the interest he has taken in learning and by the motivation he has shown in educating himself, inside and outside of school. Of particular value is what he has done to educate himself since leaving school.

Has he taken night-school, correspondence, or business courses which would help him improve himself? Or has he developed the attitude that once he finished his formal schooling, he had finished his education?

Many great men who influenced our civilization had no university training; some had very little formal education. This does not mean that they were uneducated. These men educated themselves the hard way in their spare time.

Anything that will help you get a picture of a man's

attitudes toward education—his motivation in pursuing it and his steadiness of effort in obtaining it—will be helpful in appraising his attitudes and motivation.

Here are some specific questions to ask in this area: Would you mind telling me briefly about your educational qualifications? Did you study hard or did you take it easy in school? Was your standing average, above average, or below average when compared with others?

Did you ever fail a year?

Did you ever come first in your class or win a scholarship?

Why did you leave school?

What educational courses have you taken since leaving school?

Hobbies

A man's hobbies reveal him doing the things he likes to do, at the pace which he sets for himself. In other words, if you can determine the way he works at his hobbies, you will have a clue to how he will work on the job.

If a man shows a great deal of drive, intensity, and enthusiasm for his hobbies, he is likely to carry these characteristics over to the job and show the same kind of enthusiasm and motivation there.

For example, here are two men whose hobby is golf. One is a casual, easy-going player who doesn't worry about his score. He plays golf because he likes the fresh air and the sunshine. He doesn't care whether he wins or loses in competition. The other man is an intense, worrisome player who fights the game and tries to win. He is very upset if his game is off. He is constantly taking lessons and trying to improve himself. He reads about golf and is a real student of the game. He plays to win. He hates to lose. He likes competition. It's a safe bet he carries these attitudes into business.

The way these two men play the game of golf reveals much about them as individuals. The more you find out about a man's hobbies and how he approaches them, the more you will learn about his temperament, habits, and drive.

Here are some specific questions you can ask in the hobby area: Do you mind telling me if you have any hobbies? Tell me about them.

Do you take your hobbies seriously or casually?

Social Life

The social area discloses important information about a man's ability to get along in groups and to take responsibility, and his capacity for leadership and teamwork.

For example, is he a man who actively contributes his time and effort to the organization he belongs to, or does he join only in order to gain personal advantage? The answer to this question will reveal much about his maturity.

Here are some specific questions to ask in this area:

Have you ever held office in any group organization?

Have you ever been captain, coach, or manager of a team in any sport?

What is the highest level of competition you have reached in any sport?

Economic Behavior

A psychologist once said to me, "Tell me how you handle your money, and I'll tell you many things about your personality, temperament, and character."

For example, if a man is inclined to be a spender, if he buys what he wants when he wants it, if he goes into debt and jeopardizes his future by obligating himself beyond his income level, he is probably lacking in self-control, judgment, and foresight.

On the other hand, if a man is thrifty, and is careful with his money, and has protected his future by good insurance and pension programs, he reveals good judgment, self-control, and the capacity to show foresight.

Each of these men is likely to show these same weaknesses or strengths on the job. Here are some questions:

Are you inclined to be a spender or a saver?

Have you ever been in debt?

On what luxuries do you spend money?

Health

When you hire a man, you are buying three things:

(1) His mental capacity

(2) His leadership ability

(3) His physical stamina

If you hire a man who is not in good health, you are getting only part of your money's worth. For this reason, many corporations give job candidates a physical examination. This is an excellent idea.

However, many facts about a man's health may be

determined without a physical examination. Questioning him about his health can be very revealing. The interviewer can ask about the applicant's most serious illness, his attitudes toward health, and the steps he takes to stay in good health.

Just as important as his physical health is his mental health. Here you should explore his ability to get along with people, his effectiveness in his work, and his general state of mind.

Specific questions to ask in this area:

What is the most serious illness you have ever had?

Do you feel that your general health has prevented you from being as successful as you otherwise could be?

Do you tire easily?

How many hours of sleep do you need each night to keep up your normal work effort on the job?

Is your present job an exceptionally strenuous one?

Would you say you have less physical vitality than the average person?

Do you worry?

Do you ever lose sleep because of worry?

Religion

It is not necessary to ask a man what religion he practices, but it is desirable to know how he practices his religion.

Does he attend church regularly? Does he contribute anything to the church in time or money? What are his attitudes toward church? What offices has he held in the church? What work has he done for the church?

These questions will reveal a man's belief in something bigger than himself, his willingness to contribute time and effort to a worthwhile cause, his sense of values and his controlling ideals. If he doesn't have a religion, what is his philosophy of life?

Specific questions to ask in this area:

Do you ever go to church?

How often do you attend?

Do you have any particular system or creed which guides you in your day-to-day work and activities?

Military Record

In the military service, you frequently find a man doing something he doesn't want to do but sticking to it anyway because he feels it is his duty. Here you get a good picture of his self-discipline.

It is important to review a man's military record to see what progress he made during those years. But equally important is his attitude toward the service. Did he like it? Why did he serve? Was he resistant? How did he adjust?

Such a review of this area of his life gives us clues to a man's flexibility, emotional stability, and his capacity to face adversity.

Specific questions to ask in this area:

Will you give me a brief history of your military service.

Did you take any special courses of training in the service which would help you in civilian life?

What rank did you hold when you were discharged?

Were you unhappy in the service?

Present Family Life

His present family life is important. Every man spends time at home with his family, and the influences, pressures, and general climate in which he lives are vital to his work performance.

His marital adjustment, the number of children he has, how he acts as the head of a family, how happy or unhappy his family life is—all these things will help to reveal his philosophy, character, stability, and maturity.

Specific questions to ask:

What did your wife do before she was married?

Does she think you will make good on this job?

If not, what does she think you should do?

How does your wife feel about your job?

Work Record

This is the most vital area of all.

Here we are interested in tracing his work history to find out what specific jobs he has done and what kind of work he likes and dislikes.

What criticisms has he received and what compliments? What promotions and wage increases has he been given? What are his ambitions?

Anything about his past work record that shows strengths and weaknesses will be helpful in appraising him.

Here you must watch for the constant job changer or the man who has never found a job he likes. You will likely find that in these situations there was really nothing wrong with his past jobs, but something wrong with his attitude toward them.

From the jobs that he has done well, you can get clues to his motivation, skills, and aptitudes. His work history is also very revealing of stability, dependability, and capacity for leadership.

Specific questions to ask in this area:

Have you been unfortunate in having weak supervisors in some of your jobs?

What type of work do you like best?

Have you been treated unfairly by any of your previous employers?

Have most of your past jobs been difficult?

Could you give me an example of a job in which you worked hard?

What promotions have you received?

Why did you get these promotions?

How often did you receive pay raises?

Why did you get these raises?

Have you ever had a job which was completely suitable for you?

Have you disliked most of your past jobs?

Have you ever been complimented for your good work?

Has your work ever been criticized by others?

Have you ever supervised the work of others?

What do you consider your best qualities on the job?

What would you say are your greatest weaknesses on the job?

In reviewing the foregoing ten areas of a man's life, you should be continually looking for information that will help you to appraise these characteristics:

ATTITUDES: Is he positive in his attitudes or does he tend to be negative? Does he think the world owes him a living, or does he want an opportunity to prove by extra effort that he is capable of assuming responsibility?

MOTIVATION: Does he have drive? Is he ambitious? Is he willing to make the sacrifices needed to back this up by hard work? Is he a dynamic, aggressive person who will show initiative and apply himself to anything he undertakes?

STABILITY: Has he shown the capacity to stick to a

job till it's done? Is he steady? Is he reliable? Does he show persistence in everything he undertakes, or is he erratic and changeable?

MATURITY: Does he have self-control? Has he been able to manage his money well and hold on to the jobs he has undertaken?

Is he free of self-centered tendencies? Or is he constantly concerned with his own selfish needs, even to the extent of neglecting those of others for whom he should take responsibility?

Is he decisive? Or has he proven unable to make sound decisions?

Is he a logical thinker or is he unrealistic? Has he shown a capacity for seeing his own weaknesses and limitations, admitting them, and developing himself from this realistic appraisal? Has he been able to face adversity and make sacrifices to get results, or is he pleasure-minded?

APTITUDES: What aptitude does he have for gaining the confidence of others? For leading people? Is he mechanically inclined? Is he musical or artistic or good in mathematics or English? What is the level of his general intelligence and mental ability?

By knowing the right questions to ask in all these specific areas, you should be able to make a reasonable appraisal of the man's past performance and behavior pattern. You should now be able to judge his attitudes, motivation, stability, maturity, and aptitudes.

And once you have done this, you will have a sound basis for predicting what this man will do in a specific job if you hire him. You will be able to judge whether he has the character and temperament needed to assume this particular type of responsibility.

Although no single area of the man's life will be adequate for an appraisal of him, information in all the areas together will reveal a clear pattern of his past behavior.

For example, if the man is lazy, this will probably show up in his hobby, social, educational, economic, and work areas. If he is immature, it will show up in his early and present family life, his social, economic, hobby, and work areas.

When you see a personal characteristic influencing several areas of a man's life, you can be reasonably sure that this is one of his well-established traits or behavior patterns.

It is not necessary for a man to have activity in every area, but if he does have activity in an area, once you reveal this activity and appraise it, you will be able to appraise him better.

For example, you might have a very successful man with no hobbies, no religion, no military experience, little social life. In this case, his job is probably a substitute for his hobby, his religion, and his social life. Because he lacks activities in these areas, it doesn't mean that he is lacking in motivation, stability, or maturity.

Just as valuable as the help this appraisal will give you in evaluating the man as a worker, is the help it will give you in understanding the man as a human being. You will know his strengths and weaknesses, where you can depend on him and where he needs help, how you can best guide, coach, and develop him into a productive employee.

Once you master this technique, and once you accept the fact that no one has the ability to size men up by looking at them or chatting with them casually, then your effectiveness in appraising men will increase.

Remember, the only chance you have to really understand a man is by getting complete knowledge about him.

This technique does not require any great skill or intelligence. It does, however, require a reasonable amount of judgment, some understanding of people, and the capacity to put men at ease and gain their confidence during the interview.

It also requires the ability to learn the right questions to ask to get the vital information that's not on the surface. And above all, it requires the capacity to interpret this information, to put together a living, breathing picture of this man in relation to his job and his life. If you develop this ability, you will find it to be a talent that will pay you dividends in hiring the right men and in motivating them.

4

TYPES OF LEADERSHIP

There are three types of leadership which are commonly used by supervisors in their efforts to guide and motivate men. We are most familiar with autocratic leadership. This was used for generations by leaders in the army and the church, and when business reached the stage where it needed leadership, it adopted its methods from these institutions.

Autocratic leadership is best typified by the fact that the leader does all the thinking, planning, and organizing, and the men on his staff carry out their duties as directed by him. The autocratic leader is not necessarily a hostile leader, nor does he always achieve his goals by forceful or dogmatic methods. Sometimes he can be very smooth and persuade men to do his will. Sometimes he resorts to bribery. Men get to know that if they follow through and do exactly what he wants them to do, certain rewards will be theirs.

The key to autocratic leadership is that the leader does not welcome any suggestions or ideas from the people on his staff. Men working with an autocratic leader soon get to know that their job is to carry out the duties assigned to them. They are not to reason why or to do much thinking. It is a handicap to be creative or to have any original ideas when employed by an autocratic leader. He expects to make the snowballs and he wants other people to throw them. If somebody else starts to make snowballs, he resents it.

Every supervisor at times uses autocratic leadership when he is under pressure and things must be done quickly. He then resorts to demanding and ordering fast action. Provided his attitude is right, he can get results with this method, in special situations.

A typical autocratic leader could be described something like this. He is a dynamic, aggressive, hard worker. He is a man who gets results through sheer drive and power. When he is around, things are jumping and people go to work for him because he has a strong personality and because he is competent and knows what he is doing. However, he tends to be openly critical of people. At times he is hostile toward them. He frequently doesn't have respect for the men on his staff, and as a result, good men will usually not work for him. They are dissatisfied in this kind of climate and they look around for another job.

When the autocratic leader goes out of town, everybody is glad to see him go. Sometimes people go to sleep when he is away and they don't wake up until he comes back. When he does come back, everybody wakes up with a bang, and his dynamic personality carries people along. He usually fails to develop leaders who can succeed him, and when he leaves, things often fall apart for a time until others develop people to assume responsibility.

Frequently the autocratic leader becomes a bottleneck in the organization because people have come to him for final decision-making. He is not the kind of person who likes to delegate responsibility and authority, and as a result, he does the final decision-making based on personal inspection. The autocratic leader is really saying "Do it my way."

The advantages of autocratic leadership are as follows:

There is usually great flexibility in the organization. One man can make fast decisions and get aggressive action. There is centralized control, which means that key decisions affecting the entire organization come from one person. Leaders of this type are often very successful in small organizations which can be run by one man.

Autocratic leadership is more likely to be successful with personnel who lack education and special training. The more intelligent and better educated men are, the less they will respond to autocratic leadership. Some autocratic leaders have great success because of their technical competence. Most men want to work for a successful organization, and if they recognize a man who can lead them to success, they will follow him in spite of the fact that he may not practice good human relations. Some autocratic leaders, because of their capabilities and strong personalities, can almost hypnotize men into working for them in situations which are not particularly good for the men.

The autocratic leader is usually a decisive man of action who gets straight to the heart of the problem. Because he knows what he wants and knows how to get it, he doesn't feel the need for any help from people in his organization. He feels that he has better answers than the men on his staff and he doesn't bother asking others to participate with him in management.

If you have a situation which calls for pioneering and getting something started in the face of great resistance, an autocratic leader is usually the best bet to get the job done. He may leave a few bodies lying around, but he will get results. Many businesses were founded by strong autocratic leaders who ran the organization single handed and overcame great obstacles to succeed.

The autocratic leader tends to remain aloof from his men and his downward communication is poor. He communicates only with his superiors. He gives direct orders to his men and expects them to obey him. He fails to consult people when developing future policies and he gives out little information about future plans. He lets people know only about immediate goals. Usually he gives little recognition to his people for good work.

As the result of this behavior people in his organization are not well informed and many will show little initiative. They will likely resent their boss, and show it in a direct or indirect manner.

Some autocratic leaders are more friendly in their approach and try to help their employees with some form of recognition. These men feel responsibility for their employees but they fail to communicate to them about plans and policies. They do not get their men participating and involved in decision making. No effort is made to share their leadership. This type of benevolent autocrat is better liked but there is no team effort and everyone tries to gain the manager's favor which he trades for their loyalty. People as a result are suspicious of one another and there is a lack of group effort.

Laissez-faire leadership is really an absence of leadership. The words *laissez faire*—in French means "leave things as they are." This is what the laissez-faire leader does. He acts as a clearing house and passes information from management down to the men in his organization. He usually leaves men on their own to carry through and do their jobs as they see fit. What he really says to his men is, "Here's the problem; here's what I want done. Use your head and do it your way."

He fails to provide personal leadership and inspiration, and as a result, things under his leadership usually go along as they have always been, because he does nothing to change the situation. He is frequently lacking in drive and enthusiasm. Sometimes he is afraid of people. He often rules by memorandums or by sending out bulletins to people on which he gives them instructions, and he fails to appear personally before his men to provide them with the inspiration and leadership which they need.

The laissez-faire leader is sometimes the man who is promoted not on ability, but on seniority. He has been on the job a long time and there is no one else available to fill a vacancy, and when the opportunity opens up for a supervisory position, he is given his chance, although he is frequently ill-equipped to handle such responsibility and is sometimes a sensitive person who tends to avoid personal contacts with others.

Laissez-faire leadership, however, is used by all leaders in certain situations. At times the most effective kind of leadership is to leave men on their own, to let them use their own heads and figure out how to do things themselves. This type of leadership is most effective with high-level people. Professional men and executives respond best to it.

Here is a typical laissez-faire leader. He is a man who was promoted because of his seniority. In taking over his new responsibilities, he writes a memorandum to all the men on his staff, advising them what he expects of them. He urges them to carry through with their duties and responsibilities. There is no attempt on his part to get out and show them how to do the job or to motivate them or to inspire them. As a result, things usually go on just about the way they were before he took over. He tries to guide them by remote control, but shows no direct aggressive leadership. Generally speaking, this kind of leadership is not effective except in special situations involving high-level people.

The laissez-faire leader usually leaves people on their own and makes no effort to lead them or to participate with them in the group effort.

As a result morale is usually low with poor production. This is an ideal climate in which the informal leaders may take over which they usually do. There will likely be conflicts between people on the staff and a lack of team work due to poor leadership.

The third type of leadership is known as democratic leadership. This is an attempt to build up in others a sense of responsibility, to let people in on the decision making, to get them involved and let them feel that there is something in the job which is theirs, to arouse in men the will to work for the objectives of the organization, to let people know that their leadership understands them and appreciates them as people. It is a positive leadership which is building up inside the person the urge to do a good job.

It works something like this: The leader tells the members of his staff what he is trying to achieve. He explains the goals to them so that they understand and become interested. He tries to clarify to them not only what he is trying to do, but the reasons behind it. Then he encourages them to think and discuss the problem. When they participate and take part, they assume some responsibility, and when they talk about these things and communicate with one another, they feel that they have something in common. The pressure to do good work then comes from them. The team spirit pushes them and they are motivated by an effort to do a good job for the group.

The democratic leader is really saying to his men, "How do you think we should do it?"

What happens in democratic leadership is that the leader shares his leadership with the men on his staff and he gains strength from this because they gain confidence in him. He shares some of his authority with the group. The relationship with his men becomes a mutual relationship which results in cooperation. He realizes that his welfare depends on his followers. As a leader, he is always fair and consistent. He gives recognition to people and avoids anything which tends to interfere with group solidarity and group success. The group members have confidence in a man like this. The leader looks after the needs and interests of the people on his staff, and they in turn look after his needs for top production.

Here is a sample of the democratic leader in action. He is a man who gets his greatest satisfaction from developing people and building men. He likes to help others and he enjoys seeing men assume responsibility and grow with experience and opportunity. He is a leader who is building a strong team and he taps the brain power of the men around him. He is a good listener and he communicates well with his men.

He delegates complete responsibility and authority and tries to free himself for planning, thinking, and organizing. When he goes out of town, things run just as well as when he is at home, because the same people are doing the work. He has a team effort on the job, which enables him to get away when necessary without upsetting the efficiency of his organization. He has developed one or two men who are capable of taking over from him. If he is promoted and goes up the line, someone else is prepared to step into his job and assume his responsibilities.

Although most good supervisors use the three different kinds of leadership, they tend to be known as either democratic, laissez-faire, or autocratic. In other words, they rely mostly on one type of leadership, although they use the other kinds when the situation warrants it.

Democratic leadership, however, is the most effective. In fact, supervisors are almost being forced to develop into democratic leaders because of the type of men we are raising these days. A generation ago, children were to be seen and not heard. The father's word was law. He was the ruler of the family and children learned to do what they were told. In those days, the autocratic leader, the old straw-boss, was successful. Men worked and did what they were told, because if they didn't, their boss threatened to fire or discipline them.

Today we are raising a different breed of men. Children question their parents' orders. They are developing more capacity to think for themselves, to be creative, and to show initiative. Sometimes they are right and the parents are wrong. Through discussion and democratic leadership, the father is able to direct his children better if he uses the type of authority which allows children to use their heads more and think for themselves. He can use democratic leadership and still maintain discipline. When a child raised in this environment becomes adult and goes to work for an autocratic leader who gives him an order, he may question this order and say, "Why not do it this way and save time and effort?" The autocratic leader will probably say, "Who's the boss here? Get on with the job; I'll do the thinking and planning. You do what I tell you." In this way, the autocratic leader may lose a good man who is creative and has initiative and cannot work in the restricted domain of an autocratic leader.

The democratic leader is capable of working with this new breed of men because he welcomes suggestions and ideas from others. He picks the brains of the men in his organization and gives them full credit for their ideas. The democratic leader, however, doesn't make his decisions by popular vote. Although he welcomes the thoughts and suggestions of others, the final decisions are made by him, after he sorts out and uses what ideas he can. All of his decision making is colored by the creative thinking and brain power of the men on his staff. If he has a staff of forty people, his department is being run by forty-one brains instead of by one brain.

Leaders must be more democratic in the future if they wish to survive. Because of the speed of change in modern business and the constant flow of new ideas, the people who will survive will be the most creative. The leader who taps the thinking of his men is the one most likely to keep up with new developments and new thinking because he has the creativity of all his men working for him.

Men are happier under a democratic leader because

most people like to be free, they like to think for themselves, to use their own initiative. As a result, the democratic leader gets more out of his men. He gets his men to say what they want to do, what they can do, and how they want to do it. When they have a hand in deciding what is to be done and how they will go about doing it, they will often go beyond the call of duty and make sure that things work. Generally speaking, the modern leader tends more and more to be a democratic leader.

The democratic leader tries to get his men to participate in developing policies and future plans. He keeps his men informed on management policy and spells out the reasons behind it. He participates as part of the team effort, commends people for good work and constructively criticizes when their work is not up to standard. His discipline is more in the form of education and team effort than in the form of punishment.

As a result men on his staff know the policies of the company and plans for the future. They know what is expected of them and why. Because the democratic leader delegates authority and responsibility as much as possible, people are more interested in their work. Absenteeism, labor turnover and job dissatisfaction are reduced and production increases.

Let's take specific examples of these three types of leadership and see how they work in practical situations. Let's take an example from a sales department, although the same principles could be demonstrated in the production department, the office, or any area of business.

In a corporation with a divisional sales office where they employ ten salesmen, sales are down compared with other sales divisions of the company across the country. Management places responsibility directly on the divisional sales manager and he has been removed from the job.

To replace him, they select a very strong salesman, a

man who has proven himself to be extremely efficient, a man who has demonstrated beyond a doubt that he has real capacity to sell. He is a top producer. He is a strong man with a lot of drive, determination, and all the other characteristics that indicate he will be strong as a supervisor. However, this man is highly autocratic in his approach to people. He is a dominant character who doesn't really respect the thinking of others. He likes to have things done his own way. He rules with a strong hand.

When he is given his new assignment, the Vice President of Marketing explains the problem to him and tells him why he thinks sales should be increased by twenty percent in this particular area. The new District Sales Manager says something like this: "Chief, it makes a lot of sense to me. I've made a personal survey of this particular division, I've gone over the territories of every man, I've studied their call reports for the last three years and the accounts that they have on their territories, and I feel that you are right. We should have a twenty per cent increase—maybe thirty per cent—and I can get it for you."

The new divisional manager then moves into his job and takes over. He calls his men in one at a time and his conversation goes something like this: "Joe, as you know, the company is dissatisfied with our performance in this area. They expect a twenty per cent increase in sales, and frankly I feel they are justified in this and it's quite possible and realistic for us to achieve this goal. I've gone over your territory very carefully and studied your call reports for the last three years. I'm convinced that this new level of attainment is possible for you if you do these things. I want you to make two more calls per day, and I am going to suggest that you concentrate your efforts a little more on some of your larger accounts. You seem to be avoiding them and calling mostly on the smaller and medium-sized accounts. I know the big accounts are most difficult to close, but if you ever click with one or two of them, the increase in your sales will be tremendous."

He explains in detail exactly what he wants this man to do and how he expects him to carry out instructions. Then he ends up with something like this: "You will find me an easy boss to work for, and I'll be fair in every way. However, there is one thing I want to tell you. I won't tolerate any weak sisters in this organization. As far as I'm concerned, it's results or else. If you can get out and produce and get the results that I expect, everything will go fine. If you can't produce, it's the end of the line and we'll have to get someone who can."

The autocratic leader, by this approach, is ignoring the needs and wants of the individual. The needs for recognition, security, a sense of belonging, satisfaction from achievement, and for being treated with dignity are all ignored. One interview has taken the opportunity for all of these things away. It has put the man in the position of being told exactly what he must do without giving him a chance to think or use his initiative.

As a result of this approach, his men are dissatisfied. They are not happy in this climate and the good men will soon start to look around for other jobs. In the meantime, they will probably get together in the coffee shop around the corner from the office and the conversation may go something like this: "Let's give this guy exactly what we want and nothing more. Whatever we do, let's not give him his twenty per cent increase in sales, or management will think he's a smart boy and we'll be stuck with him for a long time. Maybe we'll increase sales by five per cent, but this is the limit."

The informal leaders take over and this man fails to achieve his goals, not because he is lacking in sales ability, education, intelligence, experience, or knowledge of the job. He lacks knowledge of people. He does not have the capacity to work with others. He is unable to get men to work for him. As a result, he has to be replaced.

In choosing his successor, management is very cautious. They are not going to make the same mistake again. They pick the next man because he is known as a person who can get along well with people. He is a man with whom nobody has ever had any clashes or differences of opinion. He gets along well with everybody. He is an above-average salesman who has produced well and has done an efficient job for the company, but his main characteristic is that he seems to be able to gain the cooperation of people. Everybody likes working with him, and he is a sociable, congenial fellow who management feels will get cooperation from his men. He moves into the job, and when he comes in for a briefing, the Vice President of Marketing explains to him what is expected.

After examining the situation in his division, the new manager says that this is a realistic aim, and he takes up his responsibilities. It turns out that although he can get along with people and he is cooperative, he is not a strong leader. He is lacking in the capacity to stick up for his own convictions. He is not tough minded. He is easily swayed and influenced. He is a *yes man* who is cooperative in the sense that he has no ability to stick to one policy but lets people push him around and sway his judgment, and he becomes a typical laissez-faire leader. He is sensitive and apprehensive, and as a result, he fails to appear in the field with his men to show personal leadership, guidance, and inspiration. He runs his division by sending out memorandums and sales bulletins. He leaves the men basically on their own.

This new man becomes an information center, dispensing policy material from management to his men. He may call them in one at a time and tell them what management expects and the reasons why they expect this. He says, "Now, Joe, you're a smart fellow and I have confidence in you. I know you can do this and I am going to leave this to your own initiative. You carry through and do your job in the way you see fit, and I know you will get results."

For the laissez-faire leader, things usually go on exactly as they were before he took charge. Most men need more demands on them than he provides. They need someone to see that they live up to their responsibilities. As a result, the completely laissez-faire leader usually fails to achieve his goals and he has to be replaced by someone with stronger leadership capacity.

In selecting a replacement for this second man, management is exceptionally cautious. They have made two mistakes and they now look around in the organization to try to find a different type of leader. They select a man who they think has some natural leadership ability. He has demonstrated his leadership ability on and off the job. In organizations of which he has been a member, he has assumed offices and responsibilities. He has been president of one large social group within the company. He is a man whom people respect. They often turn to him for advice and counsel. People seem to have confidence in him. Although he is not a top producing salesman, he is better than average, and management feels that he has the natural leadership ability required to do this job.

When he is being briefed by the Vice President of Marketing for his new responsibility, his conversation goes something like this: "Mr. Johnson, your goals for this district make sense to me. I've looked over the situation and studied the potential of the territories of each salesman, and I believe it is possible to get a twenty per cent increase in business here next year. What I am mostly concerned about is this. I wonder what my men will think. Will you come down when I have my opening sales meeting next Monday morning and explain to my salesmen, as you have to me, why you think it is reasonable that we should attain these goals. Fill them in on the background, give them the reasons why.

The Vice President of Marketing agrees to do this, and after he has addressed the meeting, the new District Manager says, "Gentlemen, you have heard what management expects from us and why. What I would like to know from you is this. Can we do it? I am asking you this question because you are the ones who will have to go out and do the selling. I will be out in your territories with you as much as possible trying to help you. The rest of the time I will be in here fighting for you—trying to get the best in training, service, and delivery to help you achieve your goals.

"What I would like you to do is think about this over the weekend. Next week I would like to talk to each of you. At that time, I would like you to tell me if you think you can increase sales in your territory next year by twenty per cent and, if so, how you will do it. If you have any ideas that will help the rest of the boys to achieve their goals, I will be interested in those too. Please tell me anything that you think will help us to improve sales and efficiency in any way."

The next week the new boss calls his men in one at a time and listens. Any suggestions they make that are practical he puts to work and makes sure that everyone in the organization, right up to the President, gives the man full credit. Any ideas that he is doubtful about he says that he will consider further. If an idea is not practical, he tells the man why, thanks him for suggesting it anyway, and urges him to keep bringing in his suggestions.

The general reactions of his men are favorable. They like this treatment. The informal organization in the coffee shop approves of the new boss because he seems to have respect for his men and their abilities. He likes them and gives them the security, recognition, opportunity, satisfaction, and respect which they want on the job.

The strong democratic leader is more likely to get results than the autocratic or laissez-faire man because men like to work for this kind of boss and they want to produce for him. He looks after their needs. They in turn look after his needs for production. By thinking about a problem, discussing it among themselves, and contributing ideas, the men become involved and commit themselves in such a way that they feel there is something in the job that is theirs. Because they have a part in the decision-making and policy-forming, they are motivated to take a more active part in achieving the goals which they have helped to set.

Of course, no leader is completely democratic, autocratic, or laissez-faire. Although each leader will tend to be more one than the other, all good leaders use a combination of the three types of leadership. Part of the secret of a leader's success lies in knowing when to be autocratic, when to be democratic, and when to be laissez-faire.

Democratic leadership, however, works best in most cases, and the really successful leader usually follows this technique of leadership most of the time.

5

DEMOCRATIC LEADERSHIP CAN BE
STRONG LEADERSHIP

Is democratic leadership a soft type of leadership? Is it weak? Is it easy? The answer to these questions is "No." Democratic leadership can be strong. It can be intelligent. It can be demanding.

The supervisor's job is to check up on the work of his men. He must commend them when they do good work and constructively criticize their work when it is not up to standard. Some men are capable of working on their own without any guidance, direction, or encouragement. Most men, however, need someone to tell them when they are doing a good job and to show them what's wrong when they are not doing their work right. If a supervisor fails to comment, good men will think their work is not appreciated, and weak men will think it doesn't matter how they do the job. If they are getting away with sloppy work, they soon think that it isn't important to do the job right. Then they develop bad work habits.

A good supervisor never lets men get away with poor standards of work. One of the greatest motivational forces is the thrill of doing a job well. Unless a man is corrected when he does his work wrong and trained to do it right, he will fail to get the satisfaction which comes from achievement and which will motivate him to do an outstanding job.

This doesn't mean that the supervisor has to be constantly spying to see that a man dots the i's and crosses the t's. He can still leave a man alone to do the job his own way, but he must keep an eye on his work and let that man know his good work is appreciated and that poor work is not acceptable.

One of the first things we learn in the management of men is that men don't like being criticized. As supervisors, we sometimes disguise our criticism in the form of constructive criticism. However, we find that men don't even like constructive criticism. As a result, probably the most effective rule for a supervisor is to build the man up and avoid criticizing him as a person. Instead, the supervisor should constructively criticize the job.

The one thing people can't seem to stand is personal criticism, and personal criticism is usually not necessary. The job is the big concern of the supervisor, so he should leave the man out of his criticism and criticize his work. The same technique applies to praise. Rather than praise him personally, praise the work he is doing.

The only time personal criticism is justified is when a person has some personal trait or habit which is interfering with his productivity or efficiency. He must be told about anything of this nature. Otherwise, he might be held back from promotion for some reason of which he is unaware. Criticizing a man for personal qualities is one of the most difficult things a supervisor has to do. But it is his duty as a supervisor to alert his men to anything that is interfering with their work performance.

Most supervisors quickly learn that criticizing a man or his work is one of the most delicate and dangerous duties they have to perform. Most men are extremely sensitive to any criticism of themselves and they are also sensitive to criticism of their work, so criticism has to be given with great care. With hostile criticism, a supervisor can motivate men to work against him.

When he finds it necessary to criticize someone, the supervisor should call the employee into his office or someplace where they will have privacy. It is embarrassing and humiliating to be criticized in front of others. He might start his conversation by saying, "Joe, I just wanted to tell you that I appreciate the good job you did on the Jones account last month. However, I must be honest with you and say that the standards of work on this particular job must be improved. These layouts are not carefully outlined and they aren't being completed on time. Here is the way they should be done, and each assignment must be completed the day you receive it."

Then he will end up by saying something like this: "Joe, the only reason I take the time to tell you about this is because I have confidence in you and I know you can do this right because you have done other things well. So let's see you go to work and get this work standard to the level of which I know you are capable." In handling a criticism of a man's work, the supervisor must try to soften the blow and yet show the man specifically how he can improve the job.

A manager must be careful when criticizing a man not to give the impression that he dislikes him. If the man feels he is disliked, his sense of security is affected and this will affect his work. By starting out with a favorable comment and ending up with a favorable comment, the manager is leaning over backwards to show the man that he likes him, but he still must demand efficient work performance.

Another important thing in criticism or reprimanding is to convince the man that you are not trying to punish him but to help him to improve by showing him what he is doing wrong. You should be trying to educate him as to how and why he should do his work right.

The idea is to get the criticism of the job across to him in such a way that he will accept it and want to correct himself and do it right. If you hurt his feelings or upset him in any way, he will not want to do it right. In fact, you may motivate him to want to do it wrong.

Avoid bawling him out or whipping him with words, because this will make him resentful and he may slow down his work in order to get even. Don't try to prove him wrong. This will only make him fight to justify his behavior. The important thing is to get him to avoid making the same mistake again, or to get him to stop doing what he is doing wrong. The only way to do this is to gain his good will and get him to want to do the job right.

Give him a chance to explain why he did it wrong. Say something like "Joe, fill me in on this, will you? How did it happen this way?" It's important not to be too critical. You can do this by saying, "Joe, we all make mistakes. I'm not worried about a mistake. I just want to make sure we don't do it again like this. Can I help in any way?" Then listen to him. Listening in a situation like this lets him get rid of some tension by talking.

What men resent most in criticism is when the boss uses it to demonstrate his authority or to cut people down to size and put them in their place. Men resist and resent this. However, it has been proven that men like criticism which is designed to help them do a better job. They will be quick to accept the boss who criticizes their work provided they feel that he is doing it to build them up and help them. This is a sign of recognition, because the boss took time to help them improve their work.

Oddly enough, men are unhappy in working for a boss who never helps them by criticizing their work. Men don't like working for a weak boss. They say that a weak boss doesn't know what he wants. He is too changeable. He can't make up his mind. He hasn't the strength to stick up for his convictions. One man comes in one day and persuades him to do one thing; another man comes in the next day and persuades him to do the opposite. Nobody knows where they stand with him. Men want a boss with strength.

One of the most favorable things that a supervisor can have his employees say about him is that he is tough but fair. A demanding boss who insists that work be done right is acceptable provided he treats men fairly and is concerned with their interests. Men want to work for an operation that is successful. They will follow a boss who knows what he is doing. Most men would prefer to work for a boss they respect than one they like. They will frequently follow a leader who is direct and dominant because they have confidence in him. They know he knows his business and will lead them to success in their work. This is important to every worker and he will sometimes put up with a boss who isn't too good in human relations because they respect his ability. This accounts for the success of many supervisors, managers, and executives.

Unfortunately, as managers, I think one of the great mistakes we make is that we sometimes shy away completely from this job of checking up on people when their work isn't right. We avoid checking up because this isn't a pleasant task. Most of us don't like being critical of others, and we avoid it because we want to be liked by the men who work for us.

A supervisor who avoids criticizing the work of his men and accepts poor standards of work in order to be well liked is letting down the whole organization. He is trying to be popular and gain good will at the expense of the company, his men and himself. Really he is being unfair to each man by not showing him how the job can be done right and how he can improve himself. He is being unfair to the company and he is being unfair to himself.

Constructive criticism of men's work is at the basis of

all motivation. How can a man improve himself unless he knows what he is doing wrong? Sometimes men go along for years with poor standards of performance because their boss didn't check up on their work. Sometimes men are fired when a new boss takes over a department. They get fired for not doing their job right. These men sometimes say, "Why didn't somebody tell me about this years ago? I could have improved." They were not told about below-standard performance because some weak manager failed to do his job right.

Not only is it desirable for a supervisor to tell a man when his work is below standard, it is his duty to tell him.

Unfortunately, some supervisors have within them a tendency to be hostile critics. Supervisors are usually smarter and more capable than the men who work for them. That's how a man gets to be a supervisor. He is the smartest man in the work group, so the boss makes him a supervisor. As a result, he tends to be more demanding and more critical of less capable workers. Sometimes his criticism comes in the form of hostility. When this happens, and he becomes a hostile critic, he interferes with the performance of his men. He can even damage the health of a man.

Men who are constantly subjected to criticism become quite disturbed and emotionally upset. Hostile criticism is a club which can severely injure the emotional health of men who work under it. It will surely motivate men to work against the boss in order to get even with him.

When a supervisor embarks on the job of criticizing someone's work, he should consider these things: What were the circumstances involved when this man made this particular error? What were the peculiar difficulties under which the man was working at the time? What is his record as a worker?

A man who is criticized in a hostile manner when he makes a mistake usually resists. Some men work against the supervisor and try to cut him down to size. Others will hide their resentment but will eventually leave the job. One of the most important things to remember about criticism is not to be too severe. When you criticize someone, do it in a relaxed manner and don't make a big issue of it.

Before criticizing a man's work, it is very important that you get all the facts and know all the circumstances. Don't jump in impulsively. Plan ahead what you are going to say and remember that the purpose of criticism is not to punish but to educate. The more you can show a man the reason why he shouldn't do what he is doing, the more likely he is to behave as you want him to.

When a supervisor loses control before someone, he loses that person's respect. When a supervisor is angry or overly emotional, the man being criticized resists. He knows that the supervisor is annoyed with him and he may interpret this as a dislike for him on the part of the supervisor. This undermines his security.

For some reason, good human relations cannot tolerate emotionalism. Most capable executives are relaxed and calm when dealing with people. Even when an employee loses control and comes charging into his office, the effective executive keeps his composure. Instead of losing his temper, he encourages the man to talk. After the man has blown off steam, he frequently calms down and becomes rational.

A good approach to criticizing a person's work is to show him why he is letting down the whole organization by not doing his job right, and how it involves not only him but other people. In many situations, men will do things for the team and their fellow workers which they won't do for the boss. The smart boss, of course, constantly appeals to this team spirit of people.

For example, here is a man who has come in late a few times and the boss has reprimanded him once. Now he is late again and the boss calls him into his office. "Joe, you have always been one to carry your fair share of the load around here, and I can't understand why you suddenly require this favoritism."

"Who says I need favoritism?" asks Joe.

"Well that's what it adds up to. Everybody else gets to work on time. If I let you come in late, I'm playing favorites with you. It isn't fair to the team."

"O. K., boss, I get the message."

One of the great dangers of democratic leadership is the tendency that the democratic leader has, at times, in picking the brains of his people, to go further and take a vote to get the majority opinion and to go with the vote. This is really an abdication of responsibility. The supervisor must have strong convictions and strong beliefs. There is no quarrel with the democratic leader's tapping the brains, the initiative, and the creativity of the men on his staff, but there is a great deal wrong with his depending on these men to make his decisions for him.

The democratic supervisor may be tempted to go along with the majority in order to keep the good will of his men when he believes them to be wrong. In situations like this, he must explain his position, give his reasons, override the majority, and make the decision which he believes to be right. When the results are in, he alone must take responsibility for the performance of his department; therefore, he must make decisions that he believes are right.

Any supervisor who is tempted to avoid criticizing his men in order to be well liked must remember that being a supervisor is not winning a popularity contest. Men will not respect him, or like him, unless he does his work right. Competence and the capacity to lead effectively are the only things that will gain the liking and respect of his men. He must never accept weak standards of work in order to be well liked, or the success of his department will suffer, and this will affect everyone. Men want to be part of a successful operation and they will respect a boss who can lead them to success.

Case Study

Bill Martin is an office department supervisor with five people on his staff, doing mostly filing, clerical work, and typing.

George Clark, a new employee, has been cooperative and friendly. People like to work with him. He has proven to be smart and has helped Bill to solve a tricky problem in systems and procedures since coming into the department.

On the other hand, George has come in late for the third time in a month, his work has been sloppy, and he has made several simple errors in clerical detail that have been serious. His work has been getting behind in the last few days, and Bill decides he must have a showdown, so he asks George to step into his office for a few minutes.

Bill closes his door and says, "George, I want to have a talk with you about your job. First let me say that you have shown real capacity to get along with people here. I like the way you have fitted in with others on the staff with a minimum of friction. Also, I think you have some talent for office work, and your new procedure for handling invoicing and factory order forms has helped this department.

"The standards of work, however, on other aspects of your job are not satisfactory. You tend to be sloppy and careless in your attitudes, and unless this improves, I am going to have to make some changes.

"This month you have been late three times. Naturally this must stop. Punctuality is a must in this department, and next time you are late, I will have to let you go. You also made several errors this month—one on an invoice which almost cost the company a hundred dollars.

"George, there is a future for you in this department, but unless you smarten up, we can't use you here. Now how about showing me what you can do." How could this reprimand be improved?

This reprimand could have been improved if it had been done sooner. Bill Martin should have given Clark a chance to tell why he was late before he started to reprimand him. Clark should have been checked before he was late three times. His sloppy work should also have been drawn to his attention as soon as it was noticed and before he developed bad habits.

The supervisor started off well by calling the man into his office and keeping it private. He also commended Clark on some of his good work at the beginning to create the right atmosphere. However, there was no necessity for him to criticize Clark personally by saying, "You tend to be sloppy and careless in your attitudes."

He should have avoided personal criticism and stuck to criticizing the job. He threatened Clark when he said, "unless this improves, I am going to have to make some changes" and "next time you are late, I will have to let you go."

Bill Martin made no attempt to educate George as to why punctuality and accuracy were important. He might have appealed to him on behalf of the team and he might have taken a more positive attitude all round.

Here is the way this reprimand might have been handled in order to get a more positive response from the man. The first part was all right down to "Also, I think you have some talent for office work, and your new procedure for handling invoicing and factory order forms has helped this department." From here on, it should have gone something like this:

"The standards of work, however, on other aspects of this job could be improved. Record-keeping is very important here and sometimes even small errors can cost us a lot of money. I have confidence in you, George, but I am going to suggest that in future you double check your work as much as possible. It might also be wise for you to take a night-school course in arithmetic, bookkeeping, statistics, or anything that will improve your ability to work with detail.

"I notice you have been late three times in the last month. Is there any reason for this? [Here he lets George talk.] The small amount of time lost is not important to me. But it is important to the other people in the organization. If others see you coming in late, they figure you are getting special favors around here. You always impressed me as someone who could stand on his own feet without favored treatment. I know you can continue to do it. George, I think you can do a good job for us and I know you will be punctual and accurate from now on. Don't let our team down."

6

GIVING ORDERS

One of the most important things you do as a supervisor is to give orders. Your job as a supervisor is to motivate people to do what you want them to do. One way you do this is to give them orders. Unfortunately, there are some things you can't order men to do directly. For example, you can't order a man to work hard. You can't order a man to be thorough. You can't order a man to be loyal. You can order him to do these things, but it will have little effect on his behavior. To motivate men to carry out your orders, you must understand them and work with them over a period of time.

One of the most important things in order-giving is the attitude with which the leader gives orders to his men. Sometimes a supervisor demands. Sometimes he requests. Sometimes he suggests.

For example, a supervisor in the plant who is ready to take inventory may give an order in a demanding way. He may say, "Next week I want you to start the inventory and work on it every night until you get it completed." Instead he may request by saying, "About two weeks from now we have to have the inventory completed. Will you cooperate with me and get started next week?" On the other hand, if he is a supervisor who suggests, he may say to his men, "We must have the inventory completed in two weeks' time. Don't you think it's about time we got started?"

Each of these methods of giving orders is acceptable, and maybe as supervisors you use all three of these methods at different times, depending on the circumstances. If you are under pressure, and things have to be done immediately and somebody wants results very fast, you tend to demand. If you have more time and are under no great pressure, you tend to request. On the other hand, if there is still less pressure, and you are working in a very democratic situation, you tend to suggest. The request and suggest methods are the most effective ways of giving orders because people don't like to be ordered and told what to do.

If you are having trouble motivating your men to carry out your orders and they seem resistant to taking your orders, you may have the wrong attitude. Maybe your men feel that you are trying to dominate them or push them around. The attitude with which you give orders is just as important as the specific words which you use in giving them. Fortunately, there is a method you can use to check your attitude and make sure that it is acceptable to your men. This method is to give orders to your staff in the way which you would give an order to your immediate boss.

As supervisors, if you could adopt this attitude, you would be sure that you were never offensive in order-giving. You would not be too demanding with people, nor make people feel that they were being pushed around. There are times when you have to ask your boss to do something and usually you practice tact and diplomacy in these situations. If you could carry the same attitude into all your order-giving, it would be most effective.

One of the big difficulties in giving orders is the fact that communication with people under any circumstances is always difficult. When you are giving an order to one of your men and he is trying to listen to what you are saying, he only gets about fifty per cent of what you tell him. This makes order-giving very hazardous. If he only gets fifty per cent of what is said, he is only going to be able to carry out fifty per cent of it. There is also the possibility that he may misunderstand or misinterpret what you say.

Generally speaking, most of us are not good listeners. Most people tend to talk more fluently than they are able to listen.

Supervisors have a defense against this. Some supervisors have their orders fed back to them. They ask the man to repeat what the supervisor actually told him. This has a twofold advantage: It alerts the supervisor to the fact that the man may not have received the complete order and that he may have misunderstood the order.

One of the best ways to get this feedback is to say to the man after you have given him an order, "Frank, I have been having difficulty recently in communicating with people. Will you help me by repeating back to me what I have said to you?" By taking this attitude, you avoid the chance that he will think you think he is not capable of grasping the order.

He will probably say, "Boss, I understand you clearly. This is what you want me to do. You want me to go ahead and design this form for you and you want me to prepare something that is going to catch attention as a direct-mail piece. In order to do this, I am going to dress it up, maybe put cartoons or pictures on it to make it eye-catching."

This wasn't really what you wanted. You wanted an attention-getting mailing piece, yes, but you didn't want any fancy work on it. So you have to correct him and say, "I do want it to be attractive, but rather than being fancy, I'd like to make it simple and dignified. Something professional that will catch the eye through its quality and simplicity. As a matter of fact, I'd prefer it if you didn't use any artwork at all."

By getting a feedback of his order, the supervisor has been able to prevent a costly error and much inconvenience.

So, by asking the men on your staff to feed back what you have told them, you will catch many errors in order-giving by making sure your men know exactly what you want them to do.

One of the techniques of order-giving in which all supervisors seem to be weak is in explaining the reasons behind the order. If you tell a man "why" this motivates him to use his creativity and his initiative, and he will frequently come up with an idea for doing it better than you would have done it yourself.

When a man knows the reason behind something, he is more willing to do it than if he is asked to carry out an order blindly. When you bring a man in behind the scenes and give him the background and say, "Mark, here are the results I want and here's why I think we should achieve them," he may say, "Well, have you ever thought of doing this? My suggestion is that you give consideration to this angle."

When you tell a man clearly why you want to do something, he feels that there is some part of this job that is his. You capture his imagination and motivate him so he will get behind the project, put his heart in it. If you just give him a perfunctory order and don't give him the reason why, he will just go through the motions of carrying out the order in a routine manner, using little imagination or initiative.

For example, suppose you have to go to a special meeting in your company where certain executives will be asking questions about your department. When you are leaving for the meeting, you say to your secretary, "Miss Jones, would you get me these files." Later in the course of the meeting somebody may raise a question and you may lack the right file to give him the answer.

On the other hand, suppose you had instructed your

secretary in this way "Miss Jones, I have to go to a meeting of top management today and these particular executives will be there: the production manager, the sales manager, the office manager, and the plant superintendent. The meeting is concerned with our credit and adjustment policy on sales. I know these men are going to ask me questions on these particular topics. What files and information do you think I should take with me?" You will likely find that this girl will come up with some suggestions that will be very helpful, and when you get to the meeting, you will have all the information needed to enable you to answer the questions raised.

Giving people the "why" behind an order is just as important as making sure that they know the "what" in an order.

Often supervisors fail to give an employee a time limit on orders or to tell him "when" they want it done. I think you will admit that "when" is important. You must advise him at what particular time you want this order completed. For example, you might give a man an order to do something for you and a week later ask him if he has completed it. His answer: "Sorry, I haven't quite finished that yet." As a result of sloppy timing, some part of a big project which is supposed to be ready on time will be held up.

You could easily have corrected this by saying to him when you gave him the order, "Joe, here is an assignment that I'd like you to handle for me. *When* do you think you could have it completed?" He might say, "I think I could have it for you in about two weeks." This would give you an opportunity to say, "Sorry, that won't be fast enough on this particular job. In order to keep things on schedule, I must have this in a week. If you need more help, I'll O.K. the extra expense."

When you give a man an order, the less direction you give him on the way in which you expect him to do it, the more you will motivate him to use his own initiative on the assignment and be creative about it. It is not effective supervision to spell out in detail exactly the way you want a man to do something, just as it is bad supervisory policy to breathe down a man's neck and make sure he is dotting the i's and crossing the t's and doing everything exactly the way you would do it.

On the other hand, unless you do at times give some counsel on the way in which you want things done, you may find men using long, roundabout methods of doing things and failing to take advantage of shortcuts which you, with your longer experience and greater knowledge, could have suggested. This can frequently be avoided by giving more instruction at the time the order is given. The most effective way to do this is not to tell him how to carry out the assignment but to ask him how he plans to do it. Then, when he feeds back the answer, you have the opportunity to say, "That's very good. I wouldn't have thought of it in that way myself, but have you ever thought of these angles? Maybe if you did it this way and added this to it, you might reduce the actual time involved and perhaps cut your costs. I am going to make these suggestions and leave you on your own to investigate and follow through."

By asking him "how" he is going to carry out an assignment, it alerts you in advance to some of the errors which a man might make before he makes them.

"Who" is going to carry out this assignment for you? It is vitally important that you make sure you are giving your order to the right man. Seniority, rank, skill, experience, knowledge are all factors which enter into choosing the right man to carry out a particular job. You arouse jealousies by playing favorites and create resentment by going over men's heads. It is important to select the man who has the authority to do the job or the skill and know-how. If you pick the wrong man, he will often fail and become frustrated. By spending a little time on selecting the right man, you often save hours of time later.

When a man is given an order, it is important that he have the authority to carry it out. If other people are involved and he is not their direct supervisor, then you should spell it out to everyone that this particular man is in charge of this assignment and you will appreciate all the help and cooperation they can give him.

The most important thing of all about order-giving is the follow-up to make sure that the order is carried out. Delegation of authority and responsibility is only partly done when you hand out the job. Good delegation also requires follow-up to make sure that the job is being done.

Your job as a supervisor is not to let things happen, but to make things happen. In order to do this, you must follow up on your orders and see that they are carried out. The professional manager knows that he must keep a string on every assignment he gives and that he should check back to see how the man is progressing. This doesn't mean spying, or prying into the way he is doing it, or insisting he do it the manager's way. Rather, it means an attempt to assist him to get the assignment carried through right and on time.

When a supervisor gives an order involving materials, money, or man-hours, he should make a note of it and later check up on the order. He might say, "Joe, how are you coming along with this particular assignment? Do you need any help?" Joe may say, "No, everything seems to be under control." You might go further and say, "When do you think you will have the job completed?" He says, "A week from Saturday." Then you know just how you are progressing. If you need more expediting on it, you can work with him. Or if he is having any particular problems, he will likely tell you about them. You might even approach him in this way, "Joe, what problems are you having in getting that job done?" This will enable him to come right back with the difficulties he is having and you can get into the act and assist him if necessary.

Another way to keep a string on an order is to ask your man to give you periodic progress reports on how he is doing. On big, important orders, it is also wise for the supervisor to put the instructions in writing just to make sure his communication is clear.

Giving orders undoubtedly is the heart of the supervisory job. From the time he starts his job in the morning until he finishes in the evening, the supervisor is constantly requesting, suggesting, or demanding that people do things for him. The attitude with which he does this is vitally important in getting people to carry through on these jobs.

It is important to make sure your instructions are understood, to make sure you know when the man will be finished, to make sure you know approximately the manner in which he will carry out your orders, and to make sure that the man has the background and the understanding of why the particular assignment is being made. Any supervisor who follows through with these methods will motivate men to carry out his orders promptly and correctly.

In giving orders, you should check on the who, what, why, when, and how if you want to get things done with a maximum of efficiency. The more important and unusual the order and the more cost involved, the more you will be concerned with these things. The simpler the order, the more people are accustomed to doing it, and the less cost involved, the less you will have to concern yourself with who, what, where, why, and how.

Case Study

Joe Smith, supervisor of the shipping department in a large publishing firm, came rushing into the department one afternoon at two o'clock with twenty-five orders which he had received through the afternoon mail. He went over to George Thompson, one of the workers in his department, and said, "George, write these orders up as quickly as possible and get them shipped. Spread them around among the boys and get some help if you need it."

At five o'clock he came in and asked about the orders, and they were not completed. "But, George, I told you to get these orders out. This was a special order and I promised delivery on them today for sure."

"But the boys have all been busy," said George. "I asked them to help me, but they were all tied up. I've been busy too. Sorry, I didn't realize these orders were so important." What was wrong with Joe Smith's order-giving?

To begin with, he failed to check the "who" part of his order. George Thompson had no authority to get anybody to help him with the orders, and Joe had given him no special authority for the occasion. He had also failed to tell George "why." If George had known that the orders had to go out the same day because they were needed by a special customer for a special purpose, he might have reported back to Joe that he was having trouble.

The "what" in Joe's order was clear enough, but he didn't check it with a feedback from George. This was not necessary, because apparently it was a standard type of order with which George was familiar.

Joe failed to give George a strong enough "when," or the problem of timing and urgency would have been cleared. Joe should also have gotten a "how" regarding how

George was going to get enough help to get the order processed.

Probably the greatest weakness in this order-giving was that Joe failed to keep a string on it and had not checked back with George later in the afternoon to see how he was progressing.

7

HOW TO DEAL WITH COMPLAINTS

As a supervisor, one thing you will get plenty of is complaints and grievances. People like to complain even when things are going well. People will usually find something to gripe about, and they will howl if anything really goes wrong. This is normal behavior. Frustrations within people cause them to be critical.

One great mistake supervisors make is to feel that only their weak men will complain. Sometimes the strongest men will complain because they are interested enough in the job to want to try to improve it. Sometimes the weak man will let things go because he doesn't care whether things are working right or not. Sometimes the weaker men who have no complaints are fearful to take action or do anything about a problem. Sometimes they lack the courage to express themselves. The type of person who tends to express criticism may also be more of a perfectionist and more demanding of good results. He may be more difficult to handle, but he does a better job.

The professional manager looks favorably on grievances. They are a means of upward communication, which is one of the most difficult kinds of communications to maintain.

Another great advantage of a grievance is that it reveals to the supervisor a trouble-spot which he can deal with before it grows into something really big and explodes. One top executive says he constantly wanders around his company looking for trouble. Not because he wants trouble, but he prefers little troubles rather than big troubles. If he can find trouble when it is small, then he has a chance to correct the condition and prevent a big explosion.

Complaints and dissatisfactions are, in a way, safety valves which give a man an opportunity to blow off steam and get things off his chest, whereas if he doesn't gripe and complain, these frustrations build up and affect his work, and when he does explode eventually, it causes something really serious. As an alternative, a man may keep his complaints to himself and develop neurotic tendencies or stomach ulcers.

In the complaint situation, the supervisor has an opportunity to get to know his people better and get to understand them. It gives him a chance to prove to his people that he has an interest in them. As long as a manager handles complaints fairly and does what he can to correct them, his men see that he has their interests at heart and is trying to help. The salesman who gets a complaint from one of his customers and goes out and corrects the cause of the complaint earns the good will of the customer, who gains confidence in the salesman and becomes a loyal and faithful customer. The same frequently happens when a boss takes time to deal with a complaint.

Complaints are a measure of a supervisor's performance. From complaints he constantly learns about his supervisory efficiency. When a man has a complaint, what he is really doing is questioning the supervisor's competence and ability. What he is really saying to the supervisor is, "Mr. Boss, you are not running this department right, because this situation is unsatisfactory." This helps the supervisor to correct things. If he looks on this with a positive attitude, it enables him to know how his performance is. It helps him to measure how his men are reacting to him and how his policies and orders are affecting the thinking of the men in his organization.

When a man comes charging into the boss' office with a violent complaint, this is a situation which could develop into a serious crisis for both the boss and the man. This type of situation is loaded with tension. There is a great deal of anxiety on the part of both people. The man has a real complaint, and if he is disturbed about it, he is probably out of control. The supervisor may resent the complaint because his efficiency is being questioned, and he may snap back at the man and try to put him in his place, and a real conflict will result. Get two people out of control and shouting at one another and reason goes out the window. A lot of impulsive things are said and done in situations like this. Sometimes a good man is fired or decides to quit.

Professional managers have the capacity to keep calm, cool, and collected. This is the most important thing of all in dealing with complaints. Keep control. For some reason or other, whenever we lose control in human relations, we arouse resistance. When you lose your temper with another person, what you are really saying is, "How can you be so stupid? You are irritating me." It's a type of criticism. Instinctively, we seem to stop thinking, and muster all our capacities to retaliate in some way to emotional behavior.

When a man has a complaint, let him blow off steam. Listen to him. He has something on his mind that is disturbing him and he is not really thinking—he is feeling. He is not going to be a person you can reason with until he gets the tension out of his system. He can be compared to a balloon full of air. When he gets rid of the air, he becomes more reasonable. When a man complains like this in an irrational manner and later gets this emotion out of his system, he sometimes becomes quite apologetic.

The executive learns not to treat people the way they deserve to be treated. If a man gets upset and violently complains to his boss, maybe he deserves to be treated harshly. Maybe he deserves to be cut down to size. However, if he gets rough treatment, this only antagonizes him and he becomes more emotional. The important thing for the supervisor here is not to treat this man the way he deserves to be treated, but to treat him in such a way as to get the most cooperation out of him.

This very simple basic rule is one of the most important in human relations. If people would treat others in such a way as to get the most cooperation out of them, the world would be a much better place in which to live. Unfortunately, human beings all have a tendency to treat people the way they deserve to be treated. This is natural.

If somebody pushes you, you naturally want to push him back. If somebody treats you badly, you want to treat him twice as badly. If somebody criticizes you, it is normal to lash out and criticize.

Good supervisors and administrators keep personal feelings and prejudices out of dealing with people. They usually listen more than they talk. They get the other fellow's point of view, and even when criticized, they resist the impulse to lash back. This type of behavior doesn't come naturally. It is contrary to normal behavior and it is something that the executive learns through experience, self-discipline, and knowledge.

The technique of good listening is one of the most important things for a supervisor to learn. If he listens, it gives the other man a feeling of importance. It also gives the other man an outlet for his emotional pressures. From the supervisor's point of view, listening helps keep the communication lines open. The more you can develop your capacity to listen to your men, the better you are likely to handle complaints from them.

Even in a situation where you are trying to motivate a man to do the opposite of what he thinks should be done, if you will listen and make sure you understand his point of view, this will help you to clear up misunderstandings and eventually to change his thinking. To deal with grievances adequately, you must understand not only what the facts are, but how the man feels. His emotions are involved. Listening slows him down and relaxes him.

Frequently, of course, a man complains about something which is only a symptom of the real problem. He will sometimes complain about some simple matter when it is something more important that is bothering him.

One of the things that causes complaints more than anything else is favoritism on the part of the supervisor. Playing favorites undermines the security, the opportunity, the satisfaction from achievement, and all the psychological needs of the people not being favored. A man will find it difficult to complain to you about favoritism, but he will pick out some little thing that is irritating him and use this as his excuse for complaining.

When the employee is finished with his tirade, what you could say is something like this: "Joe, I am very concerned about this problem that is bothering you. My job is to clear up problems. However, before I can clear it up, I must get the facts. Is anything else worrying you? If so, please tell me."

During a complaint is one time when a supervisor may learn what the men on his staff are really thinking. Most of the time, they won't tell him this. Occasionally, if they lose control and start talking, they will say what they really think. This is the supervisor's chance to get the facts. A good supervisor will often encourage a man to be critical. In this way, the supervisor may learn some truths that can help him to improve his whole department. When he does feel that he has all the facts, it is important for him to restate the man's position. He might say, "John, this is what I understand is troubling you. As I see it, this is your problem. Have I got it right?"

The supervisor must be careful, in dealing with a complaint, not to make a snap decision and later find that he has made a mistake. He must not give an answer on which he will eventually have to reverse himself. If the complaint is a simple one and the solution is obvious, he should clear the matter up right away. He should correct the working condition or whatever is bothering the employee so that this sore can be healed and the man can get back to being a productive worker as quickly as possible.

However, if it is something about which he is in doubt, he should ask for time to get all the facts. He should say something like this: "John, this is very important. It is disturbing to me to find this situation. I didn't realize it was happening. If you will give me until tomorrow, I'd like to investigate it further. In my investigations, I want to talk with other people. Perhaps I'll visit the scene where this thing happened. I want to be sure my facts are right, and when I have all the facts, I will give you my decision."

If the supervisor is unable to clear up the situation, he must explain why. He must tell his employee that it is a matter of company policy and it affects other people, or the budget will not allow the expenditure now, etc. He must make it clear that the decision is his and that he stands behind it and concurs with it. Otherwise he will lose the respect of this man.

One of the worst things a supervisor could say would be, "Joe, I agree with you, but this is the way management wants it." This weakens his position. It makes him look like a messenger boy. It makes the man feel that he shouldn't have come to the supervisor with his complaint in the first place and that he should have taken it to somebody higher up the line. He may feel that the supervisor is insincere and is trying to smooth things over by blaming somebody else.

It is important that the supervisor convince the man that the settlement is fair and give him the reasons why. However, you shouldn't oversell. If you do, he may feel that you have a guilty conscious about treating him a little unfairly, and therefore, you are going out of your way to smooth things over and make him accept something which is wrong.

One good technique which is sometimes effective in getting men to think and see the supervisor's point of view is to say, "Joe, here is my problem. I am responsible for production. I have no desire to have you working the overtime that has been required of everybody, but I am going to ask you now what you would do in my position. We had to get that increase in production, and I felt that the fairest way was for all of us to work one hour extra. I felt that by spreading it out this way we could solve the problem. Maybe there is a better solution. What would you suggest? How would you handle it?" Then listen to his criticisms and suggestions. Maybe then you can reason with him and get him to see your point of view.

It is very important that you are clear in your own mind as to why you can't give him what he wants. It is important to maintain his good will. Anything that you do to make light of the complaint is going to hurt his feelings and make him think you don't care. You should go all out to prove to him that you are interested and sincerely trying to solve this problem. You must take into account all the possible reasons he has and try to see his point of view. You should tell him you appreciate him telling you about it.

Tell him that you appreciate his frankness and that when he has anything else on his mind, he should come and tell you how he feels about it. This is the only way you have of knowing how people are reacting. You want people to communicate with you and express their opinions.

In most grievance situations, there is a great deal of anxiety involved. The man is upset and he is quite emotional. He may fear that he is going to lose the respect of others. He may feel that he is being unfairly treated and he may feel that he is being discriminated against. Anything you can do to reassure him and make him feel that nobody is against him, that he is getting as fair treatment as anybody else, and that the opportunities for him are similar to those for other people in the organization will be appreciated by him.

Fair treatment to everyone, consistent firm discipline, and the handling of grievances in such a way that you show an interest in people and convince them that they are getting fair treatment is vital to your success as a supervisor.

Case Study

Joe Lory is vice president of a medium-sized manufacturing organization. One day Tom Martin, one of his supervisors, comes rushing into his office, obviously in an agitated state of mind. Tom says, "Joe, I just can't carry on with this situation any longer. I am fed up. I am the only man in this company that seems to work any overtime. Every year at this time, for three weeks, I have to work five or six hours overtime every night to get these cost reports prepared. It's too much; it's getting me down, and I just can't take it any more."

Joe looks at him with an understanding look and says, "Tom, relax and take it easy. Tell me all about it. These reports are very important, and I know that you are the only man in the company who is competent to O.K. them, but honestly I didn't realize they made the pressure so great."

"Well, it's just at this particular time of the year. Every year, about three weeks before you want these cost figures, I have to work every night until about midnight. I wouldn't mind so much, but no one else around this organization ever seems to work overtime but me. I am also questioning whether I'm getting any credit for doing this job."

"Tom, is there anything else that is bothering you? Please get it all out. I'd like to look into this and investigate it and see if there is any way in which we can ease the pressure on you. You know, I have the responsibility for getting work out around here, but I'm not trying to make things difficult for you. I'd like to make it as easy for you to do your work as possible."

"No, there is nothing else bothering me; it's just these reports that I have to prepare every year at this time."

"Well, first of all, the reports are necessary. We need them. When the new models come out each year, the cost figures have to go up to top management as fast as we can get them there so that they can set their prices for the next season. But let me look into this. My understanding of this situation is that each year it takes you three weeks of overtime work every night to get those figures prepared. You have nobody else in the act helping you with this and you are carrying the whole load yourself. Is that correct?"

"Yes, that's true."

"All right, I'll investigate. You come back tomorrow afternoon, and I'll have the answer for you."

The next day, Joe Lory goes down to the department, interviews a few people, and looks up the records. He studies the amount of work that is involved in the preparation of the cost reports which he never realized were such a strain on one of his staff. He comes to the conclusion that Martin is right. He has been taking on a big assignment. However, he also finds out that it is partly Martin's fault. He has an assistant, Jim Rogers, who is a very capable man and very ambitious, but Martin has never tried to delegate much work to him.

The next day when Martin comes in to see him, Lory gives him this answer:

"Tom, I've looked into this overtime situation of yours and I find that you are right. It has been a little unfair of us to expect you to do all this work yourself. Nobody else can take responsibility for this work but you; however, I am going to suggest that you delegate some of the detail to Jim Rogers. You might even get him to do it all and you just check on his work.

"The only way you are going to be able to avoid the pressure is to delegate some of the detail. I can't give this responsibility to anyone else because nobody else has the know-how to do it. Anyway, Rogers is a bright boy who wants more responsibility and this is a place where you should be able to give him some. Why don't you try it?"

"Well, I hadn't thought that he could do this work, but I see what you mean. Maybe I could let him do some of the detail and then I could check his work. I'll give it a try. If he could work on this every other night, it would relieve me of a great deal of pressure."

8

PERFORMANCE APPRAISAL

Many names have been used to describe the formal annual, semiannual, quarterly or monthly get together between the boss and each man on his staff. Some call it a review, some call it coaching, but mostly it is known as the performance appraisal.

On paper, the performance appraisal looks like the perfect tool to help the supervisor motivate his men. It is supposed to work like this. The supervisor's job is to develop men who do the work for him. In order to develop his men, he must keep them growing and stretching to improve themselves. The performance review is an excellent technique to assist him in this goal.

At least once a year, the supervisor should sit down with each man on his staff individually and discuss such things as how he is doing on the job, how he likes his work, what he thinks his opportunities for advancement are, what dissatisfactions he has, and what his ultimate goals are. The supervisor tells the man what he thinks of his performance, what he believes his opportunities are, where he is strong, where his weaknesses lie, and what the man can do to improve himself. Once they have a meeting of the minds and have some realistic thinking and agreement on the man's strengths and weaknesses and what he can do to develop himself, following through on this program can be a real motivating force. This information is put down on paper and a copy is given to the man and a copy goes in the file. Sometimes the man and his boss both sign it. This paper is the starting point for the next performance review.

The man should be notified a few days ahead of the review so he has time to do some soul-searching and thinking. The purpose of the interview should be explained to him, with particular emphasis on how it can help him to communicate with management.

The performance review is based on the theory that once a year every man is entitled to know where he stands with the boss and the company. He is entitled to know such things as how he is doing on the job, what management thinks of his work, how he can improve himself, what things he should try to change about himself in order to do a more efficient job, what opportunities there are for him in the organization, what he should do to prepare himself to achieve his goals, and what his limitations for advancement are, if any.

There is a real difference of opinion among supervisors as to the effectiveness of the performance review. Those who have used it extensively and for a long time find it to be very helpful in developing men. On the other hand, there are supervisors who don't want to use the performance review. Their thinking goes something like this. Nobody ever did this for them, so why should they do it for somebody else? They have constant informal contact with their men and know what they are thinking, so what's the use of adding this additional routine? Some supervisors are reluctant to use this technique because they don't know how to go about it. They feel rather awkward and shy in talking to men with whom they work very closely about such things as their job performance and the supervisor's opinion of it.

These are just excuses for not attempting to use a technique which could be very helpful to a manager in

his work of motivating and developing people. Some supervisors admit that the performance review is one of the most
difficult things they have to do in their job. However, after
they have done it a few times, they become more skillful,
and as time goes by, they begin to notice the advantages.

In practice, of course, some supervisors find that it is
very difficult to appraise men's performance accurately and
sometimes find that it is particularly difficult to tell men the
negative things about themselves. Sometimes they find that
they build men up too much and there isn't any place in
the company for them to go. However, all these things
indicate the importance of letting everyone know where he
stands, what his potential is, and what his limitations are.

This is a question of facing a man with reality now
rather than when he expects a promotion and doesn't get
it. When the boss tells him the reason he didn't get the
promotion, he will probably say, Why didn't you tell me
that ten years ago and I might have improved myself?

The performance review provides an opportunity for
the supervisor to constructively criticize a man on certain
attitudes or work habits which he may find it difficult to do
during the normal work day. However, the review should
not be negative in its general approach, but rather a positive attempt to help the man grow and develop. It should
place particular emphasis on work performance and job
achievement. The man should be appraised on the basis of
his performance on the job rather than on his personality
or temperament. The review should not be a substitute for
the day-to-day constructive criticisms and commendations
of men's work. It is rather an additional appraisal of their
work.

The performance appraisal is also one of the better
ways of improving communication between the man and
his boss. As you know, sometimes you can work very closely
with people day-to-day on the job and yet have very little

real communication with them. The performance review gives you an opportunity to sit down with a man in a situation where he feels free to ask questions about things that normally never come up in the daily routine. It gives the boss a chance to make comments on things he usually doesn't have an opportunity to talk about. It can be combined with a counseling and coaching session, and the ultimate result should be helpful to both the man and his boss.

It is important that the performance-appraisal form be designed in such a way that the supervisor is forced to be realistic. The form should provide a place for favorable comments and for constructive criticism. It should require an appraisal of the man's weaknesses as well as his strengths, and should not permit a supervisor to just rate a man fair, good, or excellent without giving reasons why.

The more the appraisal can be backed up by actual performance records, the better it will be. It should be a critique of his actual job production record. The less it leaves to the opinion of the supervisor and the more it concerns itself with actual performance, the better. The appraisal should also rate men on their attitudes and their general approach to the job.

To do the appraisal right, the manager should try to see the man's point of view and put himself in the man's place. He should try to listen and let the man talk, in order to find out how he feels about his job and why. The man should be commended for the good work he has done, and the supervisor should find out why he has failed to reach certain goals and see if he can help the man to work toward improved future performance.

Getting him to talk is vital. Keep calm and relaxed, don't resent his opinions or get into arguments with him. Listen very carefully to his point of view, then calmly point out where it is unrealistic, if necessary. Keep asking him what he thinks and end up by stating his point of view as clearly as possible to make sure it coincides with his opinion of it.

During the appraisal interview, you should be specific about the standards you expect the man to meet on the job in the next year. What improvements do you want him to make in terms of increased efficiency and output?

In regard to his self-development program for the next year, it should be as specific as possible. What courses should he take, what group organizations should he join, what reading should he do, and what other specific projects will be of help to him?

You should give him a chance to raise any questions that are on his mind. Here you could ask for his opinions and suggestions for work improvement.

His future plans should also be discussed. What are his goals? Are they realistic? If so, in what way can he develop himself to achieve these goals? A very important part of the appraisal is to bring realism into the picture. If he is overly optimistic about his future advancement, he must be told why. You must be careful not to discourage him from trying for bigger things; at the same time, don't promise him anything which you may not be able to live up to later.

The performance appraisal should be an exchange of ideas which help man and boss to understand one another better and to achieve their goals. The boss should be open to suggestions as to how he can help the man improve himself. Maybe the man would like to have more responsibility and to do more on his own. Maybe he wants more coaching, guidance, or training from the boss, or he may feel that the supervision he is getting is too close. The manager should be open minded about how he can improve his attitude toward the man and his guidanec of him.

The result of the interview should be summed up in such a way that the man and manager agree on the appraisal and a program for the man's future development. He should be motivated to try to improve himself. The appraisal should be put down on paper and become the basis of the next review. The interview should end on a friendly note with the understanding that the man can talk to his boss further at any time.

Case Study

An office manager has arranged with one of his department supervisors for the annual performance review. The supervisor was advised a few days ahead of the appointment time and he comes in to meet with his boss. They sit down together in the manager's office. He might open up by saying, "Charlie, how are things going in your department? I wish you would tell me how you feel about your job performance, how well you are doing, and how you think you could improve things."

The department supervisor then might say, "Well, Mr. Jones, as a matter of fact, I think I have been doing very well. I feel pleased with the way my department has taken a surge ahead in productivity."

Mr. Jones then says, "Yes, I think you have improved things. How were you able to do so well last year—your output is up twelve per cent."

"Well, I'm a hard worker, and by putting a lot into the job, I am getting results. As far as the future is concerned, I am aiming for your job as soon as you have moved up the line."

"Charlie, I think it is very healthy that you are aiming for my job and I would like to see you get it. The only problem is that I have four other supervisors on the same level as you who are all aiming for my job. My only concern is that the best man get it, the man who is most capable of doing a good job for the company.

"As far as your appraisal of your work is concerned, I

am inclined to agree with most of the things you say. I do think you are a hard worker; every time I come down to your department, I notice you are busy working and I think you are under quite a bit of pressure. One suggestion I might make is that I think you are doing too much work yourself and not delegating enough to the people in your department. Your men sit around too much and don't do as much as they should. My suggestion is that you learn more about the technique of delegating. I would even go so far as to suggest that you could develop yourself in the area of leadership. I think you have leadership potential but probably haven't developed it. I would like to see you getting your department organized in such a way that you will be doing less detail work and more organizing, planning, and motivating of your men."

"I hadn't thought of it this way, Mr. Jones, but maybe you are right. Maybe I could improve in this direction, and I'm open-minded to suggestions. What did you have in mind?"

"Well, I think there are a couple of ways in which this could be attacked. First, I think you could take a course of some kind. I suggest a course in public speaking or salesmanship or something in the supervisory area. Anything that will help you to express yourself better, communicate better with people, and develop your talents for leadership will be a definite help to you.

I think the other thing that would help you is to join a club. Either a professional organization or an association or a service club. In this club, I would like to see you go to work, serve on committees, and get elected to office. My reason for this is that exposure to men in other fields of business will be helpful to you. I also think that by practicing your leadership off the job you will be able to develop yourself, your leadership potential will increase, and this will help you on the job."

"I never thought of that. I think you have a good idea.

I am interested in doing anything that will help me to develop."

"Let's put some of these things down on paper, Charlie, and lay out a program, since we have had a meeting of the minds on this. If I don't spell it out clearly, I want you to come and tell me and we will get something on which we both agree. I appreciate the good work you are doing in your department. However, my job is to help you to develop and improve yourself, so that you will be the most valuable person possible to yourself and this organization. I really think we have something here that will help you do that."

"O.K., boss, that's all right with me."

So now Mr. Jones puts it on paper and lays out the plan for next year's program of improvement. He gives a copy to the man and keeps a copy for himself.

A year goes by and some action may have been taken by Charlie on the program. When the time arrives for the next performance review, the two men arrange to meet again in the boss' office. The boss opens up and says, "Well, Charlie, you will recall our last meeting a year ago in which we lined up a program that you agreed would be good for you. I've heard some things about how it worked out, but I'm curious to hear the full story today."

"Well, the course didn't work out too well to be honest with you. I enrolled, as you may know, in a supervisory training course down at the University, but I was disgusted with it and halfway through I quit. It was completely theoretical. The man who was conducting the course had no practical experience whatsoever, and most of the people in the course were schoolboys who were not supervisors but were aiming to move up the line. I felt that the whole thing was unrealistic and a waste of time, except that I did get a good reading list on supervisory topics.

"I have bought several of the recommended books, which I have added to my library. I have subscribed to a technical journal on supervision and I have borrowed certain other books on the subject from the public library. This has done me a lot of good because I have picked up quite a bit of knowledge. I find that by spending the time in reading and study that I was spending on the course, I get more value out of my time."

"That's good, but I am sorry to hear that the course didn't work out. Maybe next year you will look for something else in training, because I really believe there are courses that can help you. However, I think you were wise if you felt that way to abandon the course and invest that time to greater advantage studying by yourself. I am pleased with your reading program, and maybe you will expand that for next year."

"Now as far as the club goes, Mr. Jones, that is an entirely different story. I did join the club and I am very enthusiastic about it. I'm serving on the membership committee and have worked hard, and I think I have done a good job for the organization. For next year, they have asked me if I would take over as membership committee chairman. I met some very interesting men down there and I believe some of it is rubbing off on me. I have learned a lot and have discussed a few of my problems with some executives. It is a wonderful opportunity to rub shoulders with men in other fields. This committee chairman's job I believe will help me to develop my leadership ability off the job.

"Next year I'm planning to take a course in public speaking. This will help me in the club. I would like to go right up the line with this club and get to be president someday. I think the prestige will help me. It will develop my confidence. I also think the public relations values will be a good thing both for me and for the company. That suggestion has worked out very well. I want to thank you sincerely for steering me in the right direction."

"Charlie, I am very pleased with this development. I have noticed this showing up in your work. You are delegating more. When I go down to your department these days, I don't see you working as hard as you did. You have some of those other fellows with their noses in the ledgers and you are sitting back at your desk planning changes in your department.

"This is exactly the way I want it. The more you can delegate the more you can free yourself for over-all supervision of your men and for running the department. Now let's talk about next year. I think your idea for the course in public speaking is good, and if you will keep on with the club, that will help. Are there any other ways that we can help you to keep growing and developing?"

With another performance-review session, they are able to come up with some supplements to the program that has already been started. Charlie goes out for another year, stretching, improving, and developing himself, which makes him feel more confident. He enjoys his work more and gets more satisfaction out of his job. This is also good for his boss because he now has a man who is well motivated and who will be ready to move up the line when vacancies occur and when the need is there for higher-caliber personnel.

9

COMMUNICATION AND TRAINING

Books have been written on the subject, speeches have been made, seminars have been conducted, and we are beginning to concern ourselves more and more with communication. One fellow said, "Why all the fuss and commotion? I don't have any trouble communicating with my people; when I want to communicate something, I just tell them." This is the way the average man reacts, and yet I think we have all had the experience of telling someone exactly what we wanted him to do and later finding that he has done something completely different. Why does this happen?

Good communication between individuals is one of the most difficult things to achieve. Couples married for thirty-five years are told by marriage counselors that they are not really communicating. They are living together but do not really understand each other. Some research has shown that when a man is in your office listening to you and trying to understand what you are telling him, he only gets fifty per cent of what you say.

This is a terrifying statistic to any knowing executive. Imagine what a small percentage is getting through to them if they are not paying attention or if you are giving orders under difficulties, such as excessive noise, or when people are under pressure or rushing to get somewhere, or when they are worried about something. The amount that is communicated depends on the circumstances under which the communication is made and the attitudes and frame of mind of the people trying to communicate.

We have all had the experience in our work of having some really serious mistakes made because somebody was told to do something and he didn't grasp what he was told.

For example, one corporation that developed a new product for sale to their retail outlets produced a test batch of this article which wasn't up to standard. Rather than scrap this substandard material, the production manager decided to put it aside in the plant until he got some directions from management as to what to do with it. Meanwhile, a large amount of money had been spent on a promotion program to promote this article to the dealers. A new batch of the article was put through the manufacturing process.

When the time came to send out the new article to the dealers in order that they could try it out on their customers, the sales manager came down to the plant with a list of dealers and the quantity he wanted them to get and handed it to the production manager. The production manager gave a verbal order to ship out this material. Unfortunately, through a misunderstanding of his verbal order, the poor-quality material was shipped to the dealers. As a result, all the money that had been spent on promotion was wasted. The article was unsatisfactory and the dealers were deluged with returns from their customers. The whole thing was a total failure because communication between two men in the plant had been weak. The cost of this error to the company in poor customer relations, bad public relations, and lost advertising and promotion effort was staggering.

In order to defend themselves against this difficulty in communication, supervisors and executives use various techniques. They get men to write their orders down on paper. They get men to feed the order back to them. Before they trust someone with a responsible job, they make sure that he knows exactly what he is supposed to do and why. It has become standard procedure in business to write down a confirmation of anything of importance so that everybody knows what everybody means.

The printers have carried this to the final degree when they insist on a proof of every order that is printed. By means of a signed proof, they can check communications and make sure that everybody is clear on exactly what the copy is to be. Even then, a man frequently gets printed forms which he claims he didn't order in this color or size of type. Even when he is shown the signed proof, he is reluctant to admit that he ordered it this way.

There is much confusion in businesses because of this weakness in communication. Some of the greatest problems are in understanding people, knowing what they are feeling, and making sure they know what they have been told to do, finding out if they are enjoying their work, and determining what their feelings are toward the company. Because of their independence, and lack of ability, or unwillingness to express themselves, some people have locked-in thoughts and wishes. Unless management knows how to get them to communicate, management will never really know what these people are thinking.

There are organizations that specialize in making attitude surveys. These corporations go into a company and send out questionnaires to its employees; from these forms, they try to rate their attitudes. For example, in the sales department they might send out a questionnaire to the homes of all the salesmen asking them what they think of the company and what they think of their jobs. How could their job situation be improved and what do they like and dislike about the organization? These questionnaires are mailed back to the firm that is handling the survey; then the firm makes an analysis of all the questionnaires and comes up with a résumé of what the salesmen think of their company, what their attitudes are toward the company, and what complaints they have about the company. The fact that corporations have to go outside to get specialists to find out these things indicates the tremendous problem of communication.

Good management and motivation of people is dependent on good communication. The supervisor must tell his men what he wants them to do and follow up to make sure that they do it. He then finds out how they are reacting, how their morale is, what they think of the company, what they think of the job they are doing. In order to make sound decisions, managers must have the facts. The only way they can get the facts is to have good upward communication from their men.

Downward communication is just as important. The supervisor's job is to keep constantly communicating to his men the policies of management and what he wants them to do. The problem of downward communication is usually simpler than that of upward communication because men usually listen when the boss is talking. People are keenly interested in any information which affects their work. They pay attention to any memorandums from the boss or from management. A house organ is one way to communicate with people. Pictures and stories of things that are happening in the company and to people will keep the rank and file informed of changes and the reasons behind changes. Future goals and plans can sometimes be revealed in this way too. Films are helpful in building the company image.

Bulletin boards and meetings of employees are other ways of communicating management policy and thinking. Constant contacts by managers who keep talking to people and telling them about the plans and policies of each department are helpful in communication.

It is vital that people be informed; otherwise false rumors can spread, upsetting morale. Changes made without explanation can disturb people so much that they will sometimes quit their jobs. For example, one firm decided to buy completely new mechanical equipment for the office, and as a pleasant surprise, they decided to install it over the weekend while the staff was away. On Monday morning when the staff came in and saw new furniture, shiny new files, typewriters, adding machines, and other equipment, they were very upset. The rumor spread that this was the beginning of automation, which would put everyone out of a job. As a result, management had a group of disgruntled employees until it was explained that the new equipment was meant to help them. Management had gone to a lot of expense to make their work easier. Nobody would be fired. On the contrary, the company had bought the new equipment to help keep the good employees in the firm.

A great problem to every supervisor is of course the problem of satisfactory upward communication. Men are often slow to tell their boss what they really think.

Upward communication may be improved by the use of certain techniques. The wise supervisor will never give an order of any importance to anybody without getting that person to feed it back to him and tell him what he is going to do. In this way, he checks on his communications.

He also uses a form of democratic leadership in which instead of telling his men how to do things, he will show them what he wants done, then ask them how it should be done. When they tell him how they plan to do it, he listens. He also has his performance review once a year, which encourages communication between the man and his manager regarding the job.

One way of encouraging upward communication is for the manager to keep roaming the ship. One of the worst things that can happen to a supervisor is that he get tied behind his desk, buried in a pile of paperwork in such a way that he never gets around to his department or out in the field with his men to see exactly how they are doing and what they are thinking. The good supervisor will constantly force himself to get around and talk to people to find out what problems they are having. He will take every opportunity to talk to people at all levels when he meets them on the elevators, in the washroom, at the water cooler, or elsewhere.

By roaming the ship, the supervisor keeps in contact with his men. He shouldn't be spying on them or prying into their personal affairs, but just going around to see how they are doing and to find out whether they need help. By constant contact with people, he gets to understand them. As a result, he can communicate better with them and they can communicate with him.

Another good technique of communication is that of the open-door policy. By this policy, the executive encourages men on his staff to come and talk to him about their problems. If the door of his office is always open, men are encouraged to come and let him know when anything is out of order and bring to his attention anything unusual in their departments. The important thing is not that the door is open, but that the manager reacts favorably when somebody comes in the door.

The attitude of the executive when someone comes to see him is vital. Is he busy and under pressure and unable to pay any attention to those who come in or does he immediately put his work down and listen and is he ready to talk with the other person? By having the right attitude and always being ready and available to talk to people, he has a communication line open that can be a very important one.

When a man does complain or draws something to his attention, the supervisor should be appreciative. He should always encourage a person who comes in to talk. If a man feels appreciated and encouraged, he will come again to discuss other things. The wise supervisor looks upon complaints as a favorable thing; he doesn't try to block them, because he knows that through complaints he gets information about things down below that he can't get in any other way.

Another way that the supervisor can encourage upward communication is by constantly keeping in contact with people at all levels in his organization. Of course, he should not undermine authority and he should use the regular channels of communication for orders and official announcements, but in addition, there is no reason why he shouldn't talk to the elevator operator, the man who sweeps the floor, the office boy, and other people from time to time in an informal way.

A good way to do this in order to avoid appearing to play favorites is to talk to anybody who is in the news. Whenever someone has won an award or achieved some goal outside the organization, like being elected to office in a club or achieving something in sports or having someone in his family win a scholarship, this can be a good excuse for the supervisor to go to that person and congratulate him. When he is doing this, he can also listen. Eventually, he will get around to talking about the work situation, and he will usually be told things that he could learn in no other way.

The annual performance review of course is deliberately designed to improve communication, both upward and downward. The manager is supposed to at least once a year sit down and attempt to communicate with each of his men about themselves and their jobs. This method of communication can be a real source of information which will help the supervisor to make better decisions.

Call a man in occasionally and get his opinions on things and ask him for advice or help with some problem, and you will get upward communication. This can also be done in a group. Give the group a problem and then sit back and listen to the suggestions that come from them. The suggestions will sometimes go beyond the specific problem under discussion, and people will start to communicate many things about the job. The observant supervisor can pick up factual information that will be a great asset to him in managing.

While these various techniques do help the manager to force upward communication, technique alone is not enough. Communication depends on the climate and the right environment. It depends a great deal on the attitude of the manager, his sincerity, and what kind of human relations he practices. You can't get good communication with gimmicks; there has to be real understanding and respect for people. The fact that the boss may be using gimmicks to get information to help him advance his own goals with no consideration for others will kill communication quicker than anything.

People are quick to sense insincerity, and they will know whether the boss really means what he is saying. Unless he has consideration for the welfare and interests of his staff, he will get nowhere. Nothing can destroy communication quicker than disillusionment with management's attitude. Unless communication is backed up by a desire to help, encourage, and develop people and to share the success of the organization with them, the ultimate goal of good communication will not be achieved, regardless of what gimmicks are used.

The training of employees requires the highest level of communication. The entire training process calls for clear-cut two-way communication. Unless the manager can communicate with the trainee, the trainee will not understand what he is to do. Unless he in turn can communicate with the manager, the trainee will not know where he needs help.

Every supervisor is involved at times in situations

where he must train people. He is constantly having new men assigned to his department. Men are changing jobs. Men are taking on new responsibilities, and they need constant upgrading due to changes in their work.

In many ways, the manager is a teacher. His job is to show his men how to do the job right; and get them to want to do it right.

The ideal manager gets his greatest satisfaction out of building and developing men and seeing them grow and assume responsibility. To do this, he must like people and enjoy his work. He must enjoy the things that he is teaching and get satisfaction out of the actual teaching process. These are the things that signify whether a man is good as a teacher or not. There are very few born teachers. Fortunately, most of the skills of teaching can be learned. Success in this area will come to the supervisor if he takes the trouble to learn and practice certain techniques. If he approaches this training task without any thought and preparation, he will fail to develop his men to the point where they can do their jobs well.

The most important thing of all in teaching a person anything is to get to know that person. Find out what his past experience is, what knowledge he has, and what training he has had that will help him in doing this new job. Certain experiences in other situations may be a great asset to him. These experiences may point to short cuts in the training process. The individual person may have a strong aptitude which will shorten the training period.

The next step is to sell the man on taking the training. It is important to show the advantages of doing the job better. Show him how he can make his work easier and enjoy it more and do a better job for the team and the company. This selling process is very important in helping a man approach the job eagerly and be anxious to learn it. It's important that you put him at ease and make him feel relaxed. You must be relaxed yourself. Don't be tense or snap at him or try to use an authoritative approach, because this will interfere with learning.

First describe the whole job and get him to see the big picture. Show him where his particular job is going to fit into the big picture, and how it will contribute to the end result. Don't try to teach him too much at once. Break the job down into several key parts. These are the points to be emphasized.

Then tell him how the job should be done. Explain it to him verbally, giving him the highlights. Then do the job for him. Show him how it should be done. Set the example for him. Through democratic leadership, we have found that if you let men participate in decisions that affect their jobs, they are more likely to accept these decisions. If they have a part in making decisions, they will be enthusiastic and try to carry them out. The same thing is involved in training. If you let the man suggest ways to improve the training method, he will accept the method more quickly.

The most effective way to learn is to do it yourself. How would you like to have to learn to drive a car just by being told or being shown? It is impossible to learn to drive a car this way; and yet if we are told and shown, and if the job is explained at the beginning, it does shorten the learning process. Now let the man do it himself with the supervisor watching and coaching. Let him do it over and over again, so that he will learn by doing. In this way, he will quickly correct some of his own errors.

Once he has done it over a few times and he has some confidence in himself, it is time to put him on his own and let him do it completely by himself with the supervisor watching. In the beginning, the supervision will be close, and then eventually the man will be put completely on his own. It's important to build up his confidence. Don't be too critical. Compliment him when he does things well and keep stressing the key points in the training.

Now you can let him do the job alone, giving him someone with whom he can check back in case he gets into trouble. You should follow up with him and see how he is doing.

If you follow these steps in training, you should have much better results than you would by just showing and telling the man and leaving him on his own. These key steps in the training process will shorten it and make it simpler.

In addition to this formalized way of training, there should be constant on-the-job training. The supervisor should roam around the department, and when he sees a man doing something wrong, he should ask him why he is doing this. Then he should explain to him why this is not the right way and show him how to do it properly. When the supervisor is passing from time to time, he can check men on certain points and correct their performance. The more you can show a man why he shouldn't do what he is doing, the more likely he is to accept the suggestion.

Training is teaching, and teaching is communicating. The basic principles given in this chapter will help you to communicate better if you follow them. It may seem more difficult than just telling a man how to do something, but the results will repay you tenfold for the extra time you spend on doing the training well.

10

COUNSELING

Selecting the right man for the job is vital to every manager because once you hire a man you can change him very little. If you could change men radically, motivation would be an easy job. If you could change men easily, all you would need to do to get top productivity from people would be to change your lazy men into hard workers, make your sloppy men thorough, make your uncooperative men cooperative. As soon as you noted a fault in a man that was interfering with productivity or the team effort, you would quickly correct it by changing him.

Although it is difficult to make great changes in people, as a manager, you must keep constantly trying to change them. You can't change the personality, temperament, or character of men, but you can change their attitudes, skills, knowledge, and experiences. And by this means you can motivate them.

One of the most useful techniques that a supervisor has to help him change men is the technique of counseling. He can sometimes change their attitudes and their knowledge through counseling. From time to time, every supervisor has to sit down with individuals in the organization and talk to them about their problems. The responsibility is on the shoulders of every manager to do his part to try to counsel and coach each man.

When you hire a man, you really guarantee him that

he is suitable for the job, and if he is not, you guarantee that you will train or change him so that he *is* suitable for the job.

One of the most useful types of counseling is occupational counseling. Here the manager is trying to get the man into the right job. Sometimes, if a man is not working out in his job and if the company is large enough, the manager can have him transferred to another type of work for which he is more suitable. For example, if the man is in the accounting department and is constantly making mistakes but has a good personality and likes activities which bring him in contact with people, there is a possibility that he might be transferred to the sales department. Or if he is in selling and finds the day-to-day duties of selling too difficult because he is overly sensitive, it is possible that he might be more effective in the accounting or production departments in a technical type of work where he isn't required to constantly persuade and influence people. In this situation, he would not have to face so many rebuffs and discouragements.

In a large organization, there is always the possibility that you can place a man in the job for which he is best suited. You can explore his real interests and find out what activities he likes and dislikes. By discovering what he has achieved in his hobbies and outside activities in the church, sports, or social groups, you may reveal talents that aren't being used in his present job.

Sometimes skills and interests are revealed that indicate he can be of more use in some other business. Sometimes if there is no place for him in the organization, a man can be counseled right out of the company.

Here is an example: "Joe, we like you and you have made a lot of good friends around here; on the other hand, your performance on this particular job is not up to standard, and I am beginning to wonder if you might be in the wrong job. This is even more important to you than it is to me because you only have one job and one life to concern yourself with and you should give a lot of thought to making sure you are in the right type of work. Have you ever thought that there may be some other job for which you are better suited? If so and you can find such work, you may become a real success." Sometimes by talking to a man like this, the supervisor can alert him to the fact that there are other areas of work in which he might succeed. A supervisor might even go further and say, "Joe, I will cooperate with you if you feel this way and I will do everything I can to help you find the type of job which will suit you best and get you placed."

This technique of counseling a man right out of the company often saves the supervisor from having to fire someone. It often saves the man a great deal of embarrassment. By searching through his past achievements, he will sometimes come up with a type of work that he will like, and by moving to some other organization, he may achieve success.

The supervisor should be skilled in interviewing men to learn about their hobbies, social skills, and other activities that would indicate fields in which they are most likely to be successful.

Another type of counseling which is useful to the supervisor is educational counseling. By sitting down face to face with the man, the supervisor attempts to educate him or change his attitudes by giving him more knowledge or by presenting him with facts. Here's a case where a supervisor finds that one of his men in the organization who seems to be quite ambitious is failing to apply himself seriously to the job, but concentrates a lot of his time in developing good will with people, particularly with his boss. The supervisor feels that the man's basic attitude toward the job is wrong and he calls him in and counsels him.

He might start out by saying, "Joe, in my opinion you have considerable potentiality for developing in this company. You have shown that by the way you handled the Acme account. However, I don't think you are using your capabilities to the maximum. I am going to be frank with you because I know that is the way you would want it. You have the capacity to get along with others and this fits you for jobs where you are working closely with people.

"I have noticed that you are always trying to develop good will with people. That's good, but let me tell you, Joe, that it doesn't matter how much we like you; we couldn't advance you any faster. We like you now as much as we possibly could and we will be glad to do anything to help you improve yourself. To develop more good will with men is not going to assist you in advancing in the organization. If you want to get ahead in your work, there is just one simple way to do it: Concentrate on that job of yours, and do it so perfectly that it stands out as the outstanding job performance in the whole organization. When you do this, you will be considered for an opportunity at a higher level, and when we are looking around for someone, we will say, How about Joe? We can't overlook him, because of the tremendous job he has done. He will likely do a good job on anything we give him to do.

"Joe, I don't think you are applying yourself to the job as intensely as you can, and I think it's because you haven't realized the vital importance of top performance. I know how ambitious you are. I know about those courses you are taking off the job and how you are trying to develop yourself personally, but let me point out to you that the one weakness in your program for advancement is lack of intense application to the job itself. I wouldn't tell you this if I didn't know you well, and I hope you will settle down and really go to work on it."

Another type of counseling might be called supportive counseling. Here the supervisor tries to lend support to someone on his staff. This may be in a situation where a man is so close to what he is doing and gets so personally involved that he can't see the forest for the trees. When this happens, his thinking is clouded and he makes decisions that aren't sound. Sometimes a little advice or encouragement from his supervisor brings him a more objective view and then he can see things from a different slant. This makes his problem clearer and gives him better perspective. One of the functions of a supervisor is to be always ready to listen to people on his staff and to help them with their problems as far as he can. This applies even to problems off the job, provided he doesn't get himself too involved personally and start snooping or prying into their personal affairs.

Here's a case where a production manager is talking to a foreman, whose productivity has slipped badly. "I am worried about your production record lately, Henry. In the last few months, I haven't been getting the top results from your department that I used to get. I thought I should have a talk with you." Henry answers, "Boss, you are quite right, my performance has been slipping and I think you will understand when I tell you that I won't be around here very much longer, anyway, so there isn't much incentive for me to go to work and do a tremendous job. I'll soon be leaving because I have a cancer and I don't expect to be very long in this world."

The boss says, "Henry, I'm sorry to hear this; I didn't realize you were sick. When did you find out about this?"

Henry says, "I have known it for quite a long time. It is just recently that the impact of it has hit me. I have this lump on my side and quite a bit of internal bleeding.

I know it's cancer and it will catch up with me soon because the lump seems to be increasing in size."

"Have you seen a doctor?" asks the boss.

"No, I haven't; I don't need a doctor to tell me what's wrong. It's obvious, if you've read anything on the subject, that cancer is the only thing it could be."

"Henry, I think we should have this confirmed. Let's arrange for you to see a doctor and get him to refer you to a specialist." By a little persuasion, he is able to get Henry the proper medical attention with X-rays. Diagnosis reveals that Henry does have a tumor. After the tumor is removed, he returns to work and is soon back to his normal performance.

This is a good example of a person whose mind became clouded through being too close to a problem. He wasn't looking at the problem objectively but became emotionally involved to the degree that he wasn't thinking straight. This happens quite frequently in job situations. By supportive counseling, supervisors can sometimes help with problems of this nature.

Nondirective counseling is where the supervisor doesn't advise, criticize, or help the person being counseled. His function is to be a good listener and by listening encourage the man to talk and get his problems out in the open. Sometimes, if the supervisor listens long enough, the man gets a better understanding of his own problem and frequently can solve it himself.

This is one of the reasons for the open-door policy in management, whereby the supervisor is always available to the people on his staff when they want to come into his office and talk to him about their problems. Just the act of talking to someone is therapeutic, and the fact that someone is willing to listen helps the person solve his own problems. This is the reason why a good friend is helpful to anyone in trouble. A wise wife who is a good listener can also be a great help to a man. She encourages him to get his problems out in the open and talk about them.

The technique of nondirective counseling involves listening, asking questions, and encouraging conversation. Unfortunately, this type of counseling is very time consuming. However, it is extremely effective. If the supervisor has some time to spend with a man in trouble, by just sitting and listening to him and encouraging him to talk, dramatic results can sometimes be achieved in solving a personal problem. We all have within us a mighty capacity to solve our own problems if we can face them squarely.

Here's a man who has a lot of complaints. He is sort of a troublemaker. The supervisor is quite worried about him, and ever since the man has been transferred to him, he has been a problem. The supervisor calls him in to have a talk and decides to try the nondirective approach to see if he can get to the bottom of the man's problem. In doing this, he just listens and tries to draw him out.

He says, "Bill, I have been noticing you since you came here on the job and I think you are a very skilled worker; on the other hand, I sense some resentment toward me. Is there anything I have done to upset you?"

The gist of Bill's reply is, "I have the feeling that I am being exploited. To a degree, all workers are exploited by their companies and there doesn't seem to be fair treatment in any work situation. Any company I have ever worked for seemed to be interested in taking all the work they could get and giving nothing. Nobody seems to appreciate anything any worker does on the job. I'm not saying that just about this company; I'm saying it about them all."

So the supervisor says, "Bill, that is very interesting. Could you explain to me a little more about how you feel?"

Bill goes on and on with his complaints and eventually ends up by complaining about his particular job and about certain personalities on the job. The supervisor encourages him to talk, and this talk goes on for about an hour and a half. Bill is still complaining, so the supervisor makes an appointment for him to come back again tomorrow and talk. He comes back next day and talks for an hour. The following day he comes back and talks for another hour, and by the end of four or five of these sessions, Bill is slowing down a bit. His bitterness and some of his hostility are leaving him because someone is listening to him.

Next week the manager has him in again for an hour session and each week for the next three or four weeks he has him back again and listens. He keeps asking him how he feels about this and that, and gets him talking. Eventually these sessions taper off to once every two weeks, once a month, once every six months, and once a year, and ultimately Bill doesn't come back any more. The answer is that he has cured himself. By listening to himself, he has been able to gain insight into his own problems and change his attitude. He has learned that with a negative attitude toward everything, he was bound to find problems in every work situation.

This nondirective technique can be extremely effective if the manager has the time and patience. Even by practicing it to a limited degree with people who have complaints, you will find that amazing results can be achieved. Unfortunately most of us in management don't have the time to use the nondirective approach to full advantage.

This is about the extent of what can be done to motivate men by counseling. Managers can try to give them support, change their attitudes, find out the job for which they are best suited and listen to them. What can be done to change men is very limited and emphasizes the vital importance of hiring the right men who don't need to be changed.

11

DELEGATION

Are you working overtime? Are you working long hours under pressure? Do you sometimes skip lunch to gain more time? Do you take your briefcase home every night? Have you avoided taking vacations for the last few years?

If some or any of these things apply to you, as a manager, it is possible that you are not delegating enough responsibility to other people. As a result, you are failing to use one of the most effective techniques for motivating men.

For some strange reason, most managers don't delegate enough. When we look into the reason why, we find it is sometimes because they like doing certain jobs themselves. They enjoy the satisfaction from achievement and the credit they get for doing the work. Occasionally men are jealous of other men on their staff and are afraid to delegate responsibility to them. But usually when a manager doesn't delegate, it's because he lacks confidence in the people on his staff.

Some managers don't believe anyone else can do the job quite the same way they can. If a man is a good manager, he is probably right. It is much easier for him to do it himself than to train other people to do it. However, as a manager, if he is going to be effective, he must delegate responsibility to others or he will find himself involved in routine duties and tasks with the result that he will not have time to perform the management duties for which he is being paid.

There are some duties which he cannot delegate— duties which he alone as a manager or supervisor must perform—such as planning, organizing, controlling, and motivating and developing people. These are the basic tasks of management, and he alone can do them, because of his position of authority in the organization.

Only by delegating can a manager develop people and motivate them and make their jobs interesting. If he continues to try to do his own work plus the interesting and important parts of the work of others in his organization, and leaves them nothing but routine details, they will lose interest and enthusiasm. The more he can delegate authority and responsibility and develop people to think and make decisions, the better morale will be in the organization, the more team work he will get, and the more he will motivate men. More vitality will enter into the total organization, and he will have time for the important tasks of management.

In a way, it's hard to understand why executives don't overdelegate, because it seems to be such a simple way to make their work easy. They could then concentrate on the duties which are most vital to their success, such as creative thinking and planning. Delegating sounds like an ideal technique and it looks very simple to practice, yet it is one of the most complex techniques in management.

Just because a man delegates a job doesn't mean that he gets rid of responsibility for it. The manager or the supervisor is just as responsible for the work which is being done in his department as if he had done it all by himself, right down to the last detail. He must be responsible. Therefore, delegating is not a technique for avoiding responsibility.

Delegating requires the capacity to understand the

strengths and weaknesses of men. It requires the capacity to counsel and coach men and train them to do the job right, to assume responsibility, and to be accountable for their work. Some executives think they are delegating when they hire extra people and give them assignments, but these same executives often keep men running back to them for routine decisions. On all matters of importance, they must check with the boss. This isn't delegating. This is giving people bits and pieces of work. Delegating is sharing management responsibility. It is trying to motivate every person in the organization to think and make decisions and assume responsibility.

The ideal situation is where job responsibility is delegated to the lowest level possible with authority and decision-making powers. In this way, decisions can be made and responsibility taken for them as close to where things are happening as possible. If he does this, a manager is sharing his management with others. He is making people's jobs interesting, and he is motivating everybody to do the job he is given to do. This has the effect of creating initiative in people and making their work more interesting.

One of the most important aspects of delegating is keeping control of the work delegated. The manager who delegates well gives the job to someone else but doesn't forget about it. He must keep a string on it and get progress reports on the job as it is carried out. In simple terms, he follows up. He establishes deadlines and performance standards for the man and sees that he lives up to them. Occasionally he may check on the man's work to see how he is progressing. In turn, the man who has received the delegation is required to keep him informed and up to date.

The ideal situation is for a manager never to do anything himself that he can train somebody else to do.

The success of a manager is not in doing the work himself but in recognizing the right man to do it, making sure that he has the training and knowledge and then giving that man full authority and responsibility for the job and letting him do it his own way. A good delegator allows a man freedom to do jobs in the way his individuality demands. He judges people on results and not on how something is done. He never tries to force anyone to do a job the way he, as the boss, would do it.

The higher up he goes in the company, the more a manager must delegate. The foreman probably delegates about twenty-five per cent of his work, and the president delegates about ninety-five per cent. A manager ambitious to advance in the organization must become a good delegator.

One of the most important things in delegating is to have the right attitude. A liking for people and a feeling of satisfaction in developing them and seeing them grow is helpful. Respect for people and consideration for their opinions and their ideas is vital. When an executive believes that his job is not the achievement of things but the development of people who will achieve things for him, then he is reaching the kind of thinking which will enable him to delegate well. He will then realize that the most important assets he has in the organization are his people. Anything he can do to develop their skills and their capacity to make decisions and take responsibility will make their jobs more interesting and motivate them in their work and free the manager for the most important things.

Every manager should study his job and find out what things other people could do or be trained to do. The way to start is to delegate as much routine detail as possible and then to delegate as much technical work as possible. There are certain things that a manager should never delegate, such as policy formulation or planning. He must do these things himself because only he has the authority and power needed. He must not delegate his authority for discipline or for promoting or for appraising personnel. If he gives away these responsibilities, he loses control and is in the position of overdelegating where he lacks the authority and power to run his department properly.

The department head or manager delegates part of his authority to make decisions but he never delegates the final authority. He always keeps control, which enables him to check on others and change things and recall the authority he has given at any time.

One of the great problems in delegating is that the man who is doing the delegating usually has more competence in the particular job than the man to whom he is assigning it, and he may therefore become a little impatient with him when he makes mistakes. He must remember that somebody took a chance on him at one time and allowed him to make a few mistakes while he was learning.

Any time you give a man a certain job to do, you take the risk that he won't do it right. In the beginning, the risks are fairly high until you have tested him and trained him and developed him. It is important that you give him a little responsibility at a time and let him grow gradually. Don't throw a big assignment at him before he has the proper experience.

When you gain more confidence in a man, you can delegate with less and less risk. If the things he has delegated aren't carried out right, the only alternative a manager has is to keep training his men more and supervising them better. Eventually, if a man cannot be developed to make the decisions involved and take the responsibility, then the maanger will have to replace him with someone who can.

One of the problems the manager faces constantly when he delegates something is having the man come back to ask his opinion about what he should do. The smart manager will develop this man by saying to him, "Tell me how you think you should do it. I don't want you to bring

me problems; I want you to bring me your answers to problems. I want you first to make the decision yourself, and
then if you want my advice, I will give it." If he doesn't
do this, he will have a situation where he becomes a bottleneck in the organization, holding up work while people
wait for decisions to be made.

Real delegation calls for building up in the individual
a sense of responsibility for the job. It calls for developing
in him the capacity to assume authority, to make decisions,
and to become a little manager himself. Such a way of
delegating and developing men is stimulating to everybody in the organization and motivates men to increase
productivity.

A manager who says he can't delegate and finds it
easier to do the job himself rather than face the frustrations and difficulties of getting others to do it is really
admitting that he is not a manager. He is admitting that he
is unable to explain the duties of the job clearly to people
and that he lacks the ability to organize the work of others
and to distribute it properly to them. He is admitting that
he doesn't have the patience to follow up and see that the
work is carried out. In the final analysis, the only way the
manager can motivate people is to delegate to them and
let them assume responsibility, make some mistakes, and
learn from experience.

The last thing a manager should delegate is a job
which requires more of his time to train the person than
it would take for him to do it himself. The idea is to
delegate tasks which are recurring and duties which come
up constantly, so that once he gets the man trained to do
a job, he is relieved of considerable work and detail.

Just because the manager knows that he can do the
job better than other people is no reason for him not to
delegate it. He must delegate it and develop someone else
to do it even partly as good as he can so that he can be

free for other things. In the beginning of course, in delegating to anyone, the manager will keep strict controls on the assignment and keep checking back to see how the man is progressing. These controls will be lessened as he gains confidence in that man and as the man grows so that he can accept authority and responsibility.

When a manager does delegate something, it is important that he spell out what authority goes with the job, and if it requires that the man delegate work to other people, it is important that the manager spell out to the other people involved that the man has the authority. The idea of course is that the executive will develop people who can be trusted to make decisions themselves, so they won't be constantly interrupting or overloading their supervisor, or coming to him for advice or permission for every move they make. Delegating is really shifting some of the responsibility from the manager and incorporating it into the jobs of his employees.

Although the tendency is usually to underdelegate, there are cases where supervisors and managers overdelegate. Some managers who like to take things easy may assign jobs to men without keeping controls and then fail to check back on them. These managers may try to slough off responsibility on other people and delegate things to men who are not competent to assume responsibility. They sometimes delegate things and then forget them.

Delegating is a state of mind. It's a philosophy of management. Unless a manager is capable of becoming a democratic leader and building up other people, he will find difficulty in delegating. The completely autocratic leader is sometimes very capable of planning work and passing out job assignments, but he is unable to give freedom of action in carrying it out. He fails to let his subordinates act on their own and assume responsibility and make decisions. There is little to be gained from this kind of delegation because men have to keep coming back constantly to their boss for decisions. They know that he doesn't want them to make decisions on their own. He wants to control the final decision-making.

Once the manager has adopted the proper attitude toward delegating, then he must choose his men carefully. The idea is to have the man who is taking the delegated responsibility feel that he is working with the executive and not feel that he is just a hired hand doing chores for somebody. Once he has selected his man carefully, the manager must start out slowly and give the man some small responsibilities and see how he does. As he comes along, the manager will help him to grow and take the work in easy stages. The manager must be reasonable in what he expects his men to do and give them time to get the feel of working together. One good way to start out delegating is to ask employees their opinions about things. When they come in to the manager to ask about a problem, he should ask them about the problem right back and get them to discuss it among themselves.

Usually people like to have things delegated to them. They like to use all their abilities. If a man has certain capacities, he finds it a challenge to be able to use them on the job. This arouses his interest in the work and motivates him to work harder.

12

TEAMWORK

The manager's job is to get results through people. To achieve this goal, he must hire the right men, then train and develop them to do specific jobs within his organization. In addition to this, he has the responsibility of getting his people to cooperate with one another and coordinate their efforts to achieve his goals. This part of the manager's motivating job is never over. He must constantly keep striving for a better team effort. Unless he does this, he will fail to reach top productivity in spite of the fact that he may have the best people working for him. A group of all stars without team effort will be beaten by a group of bums who are working as a team.

There are specific things that a manager can do to inspire teamwork, but unless the basic climate and working conditions are right, he will not get the results he wants.

The key to teamwork is the cooperation of people, the desire on their part to want to do a good job. This attitude on the part of employees can only be obtained by making sure that their needs, both basic and psychological, are looked after.

To develop teamwork, the manager must be a leader. He must treat people fairly and give them credit for work well done. He must know his job. If he is incompetent, people will have little confidence in him. If he is competent, they will respect him and will not always object to a demanding approach because basically men want to be identified with a successful operation and they are quick to recognize a man who can lead them to success.

The more he can get his people into the act by practicing democratic leadership, the more they will feel that they are part of the team. The manager must delegate and give full responsibility and authority and try to develop people to assume it. When he trusts people, they will respond and be more cooperative. Important also is his ability to communicate to people what he wants them to do and to tell them how he appreciates what they are doing.

The good manager must check up on people who are not contributing to the team effort. He must not let people get away with sloppy work that affects others. He must be demanding in regard to cooperation if he wants to get his men striving to do a good job. Those who don't cooperate must be counseled and coached, and all attempts must be made to improve their attitudes and efforts; but if a man seems unable to fit his work into the group effort, he must be removed from the group or he will destroy the team spirit.

Good principles of organization are very important in team work. Organizing a team is a full-time job and it can't ever be relaxed. The manager must constantly evaluate the effectiveness of people, not only in achieving their goal, but in cooperating with the organization as a whole. In addition to good organization and good communication, good planning is necessary for teamwork. Unless management plans ahead and knows exactly what those plans are, it is very difficult to get the group functioning as a team. The manager must communicate his plans to the team and follow up to see that they are being carried out. He must see that people are coordinating and cooperating in an effort to get results.

This is the background required in any situation where teamwork is necessary. In addition, there are specific techniques involved in getting teamwork. The best way to learn about teamwork is to look at the great teams in sports. Those that achieve that magic coordination of effort do it by teamwork. The great football team is the ideal example.

When we study this professional team effort, we must admit that the most important thing in teamwork is having a purpose. The purpose of course in football is to win games. The greatest teams of all are those where every man is dedicated to the purpose of winning the game and forgets about his own personal stardom. In addition to the purpose of winning, the pros have a bigger purpose: to play the game well and in every way to set an example in good sportsmanship. This is the big purpose.

The teamwork achieved will be in proportion to the ability of the manager to get his men dedicated to the purpose of the organization and stop pursuing their own selfish goals. The higher level the purpose, the more it is likely to inspire men and make them want to achieve it.

In business, the purpose is to achieve efficiency, production, and profit. This purpose is vital to the survival of any business. However, to get men really excited about their work, it is important to have a big purpose; the ideal is something that renders a service or contributes something to the community. Men are more likely to get excited about something that helps their fellow men than they are to be excited about making a profit for the owners or the shareholders of the company. Both purposes must be brought into teamwork. There are certain people who are service minded and will strive harder to achieve the purpose that is big and calls for a dedicated effort.

The purpose should be a moral one, and if it has some social significance, it will have more appeal. We saw the greatest team effort in history during World War II, because the purpose was big. Saving the world for democracy was an ideal that men would dedicate their lives to achieve. Men made unbelievable sacrifices and went beyond the call of duty in order to achieve the big purpose of saving the world and yet there was no money profit involved for most of them.

In business, it is difficult to find a purpose as great as this, but every business must give a service to its customers, and the more the service aspects of this purpose can be spelled out, the stronger appeal it will have. What is the purpose of your business? What service does it render to the business community? If this can be spelled out to the employees and they believe that they have a big purpose to achieve and an opportunity to contribute something, it will inspire them to work together.

The big purpose plus the immediate purpose of making a profit or getting out production are the keys to teamwork. The manager's job of course is to keep the purpose alive. He must keep people constantly aware of the purpose and keep them struggling to achieve it. If people aren't constantly aware of the purpose, they go off trying to achieve their own little purposes, which are to advance their personal ambitions or put special effort into doing things on the job which don't contribute to the over-all achievement of the company.

The only way to avoid having individuals pursue their own selfish interests at the expense of the enterprise is to have the company purpose spelled out. The company creed is an attempt to express the purpose and philosophy of the company. For example, in the company creed, or statement of objectives, we might find this kind of a statement: "The first obligation of the company is to supply the community with the best service possible; the second is to make a profit; and the third is to make the company a first-class place to work, where the personal worth of employees is recognized and they are given the security and opportunity they need to do a good job. Fourth is to maintain good citizenship as a corporation, and fifth is to aim for growth and strength in the future." A creed like this is a definite statement of the purposes of the company.

Once the big purpose and the specific purpose of profits or efficiency have been established, it is important to let people know how they are progressing and achieving these purposes and what they are contributing. They want to know where they fit into the picture and what they are doing to achieve the goals.

It's important for teamwork that each man know as much about the over-all operation of the company as possible. What does the company manufacture? He should know what the final product is and how it is used by the customer. Each man should know the connection between his work and the work of other people. He should know how the company is progressing and what the score is. I think you will admit it would be rather a dull football game to watch if there was no score being kept. This indicates the importance of letting people know how we stand in achieving the goals and aims of the organization.

The manager must spell out to each employee the importance of his job. Give him the big picture. One helpful way to do this is by drawing up an organizational chart and then emphasizing on it the importance of his department and how if the men fall behind, it will affect the total output of the whole company. If each individual worker in the department is producing, it helps the output of the particular department and the whole organization.

Each man needs to be constantly reminded of his place in the department and in the organization. You can do this by making up a work schedule and keeping him informed of his progress. Keeping him up to date on anything that will interest him is also helpful. Any publicity releases in the newspapers about the company, or any advertisements, should be sent to him because this helps him to keep in mind the over-all picture of what the company is doing.

It is very important that the meaning of his job be explained to him and its relation to the over-all goals. You must show him how he is contributing to the final product. Make him feel that his work is important and vital. It's not just the little job that he is doing but the big help to the total effort that he is producing which counts.

This girl isn't just punching a typewriter, she is one of the most important communication links between the company and its customers, and if she didn't type up those invoices and statements, no money would come in and the business wouldn't be able to operate. The more you can get her excited about her job and make her feel it's important, the more she is likely to be on the team.

In spelling out the score to people, let them know how their particular department is doing compared to over-all company efficiency. What are the total over-all company sales and what are the sales in this particular department? What are the prospects for the year? The more we can show where the product is being used and what satisfaction people are getting from using it, the more people will be interested.

It is just as important that you listen to people and let them tell you how they are doing. A manager has a lot to tell his people and they have a lot to tell him. One of the best ways to encourage teamwork is to call conferences and get people together to contribute ideas. What is the problem? What can they do about it? Keep reminding them of the purpose and its relationship to the total company output. Anything that contributes to the total production is cause to call people together for their ideas, reminding them that they are on the team. Keep using team words, by saying, "We are doing this" and "We are planning this." Don't ever let them forget that they are on the team. Ask them if they can help the team by giving you ideas.

Sometimes praise can be given in such a way that it involves a team effort. Praise a man for his good work, but praise him particularly for what he contributes to the over-all goals of the company. Tell him what he contributed to getting "our" quota or achieving "our" efficiency for the last month. Sometimes praise him in front of his fellow workers so they will get the idea of teamwork, and encourage other people to join in and compliment him for the good work he has done in helping you to achieve the goals of the organization.

Do you have these problems in your department? Do you have some people who are sloppy and careless? Who take short cuts and don't do a thorough job, who chisel and take advantage of their position? Who pass the buck and refuse to make decisions? Who do what they are told but won't do anything beyond this? Who won't help others with their work? If you have any of these problems, then you have team problems, and the only way to solve these problems is to get people working together as a team. This is a never-ending job.

No matter how good your workers get, no matter how efficient they are at their jobs, they will never get to reach the ultimate in teamwork. The only way the manager can hope to get them anywhere near it is to keep constantly coaching, motivating, and guiding them toward achieving the purpose of the organization.

13

DISCIPLINE

Every manager has to be careful not to create an environment in which the whole purpose is to enforce the rules or show power or authority. The purpose of discipline is to create a climate in which everyone can work toward the goals with rules that are fair to everyone.

Generally speaking, men want to work in a situation where discipline is reasonably strict. Men don't like working in an environment where discipline is too soft or easy. They like to know the rules. They like to know where they stand. They like consistency. It's very important to everybody to have a successful operation. Men know that they are most likely to have a successful operation in a situation where the boss is a bit demanding and where the rules are made to be obeyed.

The idea is to have an environment in which discipline is an educational process by which all people are shown how it is to the greatest advantage of the total group that everyone obey the rules, even though sometimes we have to cut back on our own personal freedom in order to be fair to others. Men are usually quick to adhere to the rules once they see that others are involved and that they have a responsibility to do their share of the rule-keeping.

It is very important that all the rules be clearly spelled out and put down in writing. Good organization and planning are also vital to keeping good discipline.

There is danger in a situation where discipline is too rigid, or where there is great fear of disciplinary action, and where punishment is used in such a way that people are so afraid of losing pay or losing their job or prestige that they become resentful and take every opportunity to break the rules without getting caught. If you are too tough with people and too punishment-minded, you build up resentment in others and motivate them against you, and discipline boomerangs.

On the other hand, if the boss is too easy and closes his eyes to infractions of the rules, people will think he is weak, and some will take advantage of this situation. When others see certain men taking advantage of this, discipline will break down and there will be a lack of respect for the rules completely. It is important that the rules are there and that the boss sees that they are enforced in a positive way. The manager who has good standards of discipline is likely to insist on high standards of work. He is likely to maintain good communication with his employees. It is important that complaints about rules be cleared up quickly and that the boss always be fair and not play any favorites. He should see that everybody plays the game.

When infractions of discipline occur, the supervisor gives the man a chance to talk. He tries to listen to the reasons behind the infraction in order that he can be fair. He realizes that his disciplining of one man is an example to others. The manager realizes that he is constantly on display and that whenever he takes disciplinary action against someone, other people are watching and they are saying that this is the way it will apply to them. The most important factor in discipline is setting a good example. If the manager obeys the rules and follows the regulations, other people are more likely to do so.

An important factor in discipline is not to punish people because they did something wrong, but to show them that they have broken a rule and rules must be enforced for the sake of the team and total production. You should not be so concerned about the rule being broken but about how this affects the total output and the fact that you don't want the rule to be broken again. Disciplinary action is a reminder that rules are important. It's also important not to hurt people's feelings or cut them down to size. Keep calm, cool, and collected and try to explain and bring the educational process into it as much as possible. Analyze the mistake when it is made to see what can be done to prevent it from happening again.

It is very important that the penalty be fair and not too severe for the offense. With a serious penalty like a discharge, the manager will be wise to get the opinion of someone higher up in the company before he takes action of such a severe nature. He should be certain that he has all the facts, that he knows exactly what did happen, and that he is acting in an objective manner, free of prejudice.

Most people readily obey reasonable orders and rules of conduct provided they understand the reason for them and what is expected of them. Most people get satisfaction out of doing a job well and being part of the team and seeing the team successful. It's only for the exceptional cases that we need discipline.

Certain people always seem to resent authority and some don't have respect for others. If you can weed out these people when they are interfering with teamwork and the activities of others, it will help. The idea is to avoid hiring this type of person in the beginning or to get rid of him if you can.

The more rules you have in your department and the more punishment is tied up with discipline, the more people are likely to resent it. This situation indicates that you feel your men are incapable of self-discipline. Train every man to discipline himself in order to get the greatest pro-

ductive effort from himself and from the group. Be understanding and firm. Men want positive leadership. They
want to look up to a supervisor as a leader, not as a police-
man, and they will respect a man who will show them what
the rules are and train them to follow those rules, and
who will let them discipline themselves without rigid
punishment.

The first step in disciplinary action is to let a man
know as soon as he is guilty of an infraction of the rules.
Not to jump on him, but to give him a friendly reminder
that his behavior is out of line. For a second infraction,
he should be taken aside and the significance of his infraction explained to him from the team point of view. If he
continues to violate a rule, he should be cautioned that
perhaps he is in the wrong job. The importance of the team
effort should be emphasized, and he should be given an
opportunity to do some soul-searching as to whether or
not he wants to continue in this particular job.

Firing is a serious step for any supervisor to take.
When he fires a man and hires another to take his place,
he is really exchanging one set of weaknesses for another.
Although the man he is firing may have weaknesses that
are interfering with efficiency or causing contention with
other people on the job, any new man he hires is going
to have some weaknesses too. The first step in firing should
therefore be to sit down and consider the advantages that
the present man has in his favor.

The man in the job knows the company. He knows
the policies and he knows the peculiarities, temperament,
and personality of his boss. This gives him an edge over a
new man. Before he fires a man the supervisor must say
to himself, "Have I done everything to help this man do
the job right? A great deal of responsibility for his success
rests on my shoulders."

When a supervisor hires a man, he really says to him,

"I guarantee that you can do this job; further, I guarantee that if you can't do it, I will train you and supervise you so that you will be able to do it." Therefore, if the man isn't working out well, some questions the manager should ask himself are, "Where have I failed?" "Have I lived up to my part of the deal?" "Is there anything more I could do in the way of helping this man, by training, counseling, or coaching him on the job?" He should explore all the possibilities of developing him before he fires him.

On the other hand, you will admit there are certain times when it becomes absolutely necessary to fire someone. If that person has developed bad habits of work, or if he has demonstrated immorality, dishonesty, or is incompetent on the job, he is going to affect other people and he must go. One bad apple in the barrel can cause some of the others to spoil.

If an incompetent person stays around too long, people will say, "How long is the boss going to put up with that person?" This could cause good men to get restless and decide to leave in order to get away from inefficiency. It is a reflection on management if inadequate or incompetent people are retained indefinitely on the staff. It is a sign of weakness in management.

There is a point where every supervisor becomes justified in dismissing a man from his job. Although this is a very unpleasant duty, yet at times every supervisor has to face up to this responsibility for the good of the team and for the good of every person employed in the organization.

The first step in firing is to make sure the man is alerted immediately when he is doing something wrong or when his work falls below the required standards. It is the first responsibility of every supervisor to constructively criticize a man when his work isn't up to standard. How can a man improve himself or hope to change himself if he doesn't know what he is doing wrong? The supervisor should have a talk with the man, show him where he is falling down on the job, and explain to him the standards which must be maintained.

After this specific criticism of his work, with specific directions as to how his work can be improved, he should be given a chance to improve his performance with any guidance which the supervisor can give him. If his work still is not satisfactory, the boss should have another talk with him, which might go something like this: "Bill, you have done some good work. Specifically, I like how you handled the Jones account. You have made a lot of friends around here. We like you; on the other hand, the standards of performance on this job are still not good enough for these specific reasons. [give the reasons.] This will have to be improved. However, before we embark on the long job of checking into what is to be corrected, I want you to consider in your own mind whether or not you are in the right job."

Sometimes if the supervisor questions the man's suitability for the job, he can counsel him out of his job and into another one and save himself the unpleasant task of firing. Sometimes when a man is confronted with the thought that he would be more effective doing some other kind of work, he will start to search around for another job and leave before he is discharged. This is much more effective than firing him. On the other hand if he does decide that this is the work he wants to do, then he is in a much better frame of mind to accept criticisms and try to improve himself.

Let us assume that a supervisor is confronted with a situation where the man says he believes he is suited for the work and wants to keep trying; then as the man's immediate boss the first responsibility of the supervisor is to see where he has been wrong. Has he failed to assume his responsibility in training and guiding the man?

The supervisor must see if there is anything further he can do for the man. Maybe there is someone in the organization whom he can assign to give him closer supervision and guidance. He should also encourage the man to do something on his own to improve himself, such as taking a course outside the company and double-checking his own work on the job. Then the supervisor should suggest a certain period of time in which the man must bring his performance up to standard. At the end of this period of time, the boss should review what has happened and see where they go from there.

If the man's performance has not improved, then the supervisor should make his final decision about firing him. He should make this decision based on the facts.

At the beginning of the firing interview, the supervisor should tell the man his decision. He should review the facts and remind him of their past meeting and of how they have both tried to improve his performance. Then he should point out exactly the things that are below par in the man's performance. In view of the facts, a change must be made.

At this point, he may offer the man an opportunity to take some time off from his job to look for other work. He can let the man tell others that he has decided to make the change. Regardless of the circumstances, when a man is being fired, his morale is down and he is in a vulnerable position. He has failed in some way, and he will likely be very sensitive. Anything the supervisor can do to make it easier for him to leave the company will be helpful. Make sure his pay is arranged so that he can make the exit easily and gracefully. Let him save face if possible.

The important thing in firing a man is not to do it in such a way that he will like it, but to do it in such a way that everyone in the organization will say that it was right.

Case Study

Bill Watson, office manager of a small company employing about fifteen people, has noticed for some time that John Simpson's work is not up to standard. John makes a lot of clerical errors. He seems to be disinterested in his work. He has come in late for work two or three times recently and his general attitude around the office seems to be carefree with a lack of intensity.

Bill Watson had reprimanded John for coming late, then invited him into his office for a long talk in which John was told that his attitudes would have to improve, particularly in regard to being more thorough in his attention to detail, or a change would have to be made. This had the effect on Simpson of motivating him against his boss. He showed a negative attitude which seemed to get worse, and he didn't show any effort to improve himself. Instead of improving in his work, he became more careless.

Bill Watson then called Simpson into his office and said, "John, I have no alternative but to let you go and will give you notice officially now, and you will have two weeks in which to clear up your affairs here and look for a job. We will give you a little time off if you need it so that you can look for something else."

Did Bill Watson handle this situation right?

No, Bill Watson didn't handle this right. He failed to coach Simpson or counsel him. He didn't tell him specifically what was wrong with his performance. He failed to say specifically what Simpson needed to do to improve his performance. He didn't follow through and help Simpson. Here is the way Bill Watson might have handled this situation.

About two weeks after he hired John Simpson, Bill Watson noticed that he tended to be careless in his work and had made one or two errors that cost the company some money. Bill called him in immediately and said, "John, I am going to be honest with you. I think you are getting along well with the people here. Your idea for changing the invoicing system was good. On the other hand, I must say that I am a little concerned with some of the things you are doing on the job. I don't think your attention to detail is good enough. You made these two specific errors which have cost us some money. Close attention and concern for detail is one of the vital parts of your job.

"Now, John, I want you to consider that maybe this is the wrong type of work for you. This is no reflection on you personally. I want you to give this some serious thought tonight and let me know tomorrow whether you feel there is another kind of work that you would prefer to do."

John Simpson declared that he did feel it was the right kind of a job for him. He liked the work. He liked the company. He liked the people. He wanted to stay.

Bill Watson said, "If that is the case, then you and I should both get into the act and do something to improve your work performance. Maybe I have failed in my responsibility in not giving you enough training and coaching. I like your attitude toward people. You are friendly and tend to contribute to a free and easy way around the office. On the other hand, I would like to see you take things a little more seriously. A little less kidding and more intensity and a more direct concern for production would help. Getting the work done and getting the work done right is the important thing in this department.

"I am going to assign you to Joe Smith and have you report directly to him. He is a good man at developing and training people; you will go to him with any problems and please feel free to ask him about anything that you are in doubt about. I suggest that we both take a month to work on this and see if we can do something to bring your performance up to standard.

"I am also going to suggest that you double check your work on the job all the time, and you might also consider taking a course outside the job in arithmetic, statistics, accounting, or bookkeeping. Anything that will help you to be careful and accurate with figures will help."

John Simpson agreed that he would do everything in his power to improve. He did understand. He accepted the criticisms of Bill Watson. He thought they were fair.

During the next month, Bill Watson observed John Simpson's performance carefully and he got regular reports from Joe Smith. Toward the end of the month, he came to the conclusion that Simpson was not suitable for this particular type of job.

His temperament was too casual. He was talking too much and kidding too much with the girls and he had a general disrupting effect on the office despite the fact that Joe Smith had checked him on this two or three times and tried to get him to settle down and take his work more seriously. He wasn't able to change. At the same time, his detail work continued to be sloppy, and he made one or two more mistakes which cost the company money. He had come in late once more during the month, and Bill Watson made the decision that Simpson had to go.

He called him in and said, "John, you remember in our last interview when we said we would give you another month on this assignment and that you would do certain things and I would do certain things to help you improve your work. You have been taking your course at night school and I have assigned you to Joe Smith, but my observances and the reports I get still do not indicate the kind of performance that is necessary for this particular job. I have made up my mind that we have to make a change. I am convinced that you are not in the right job. You are a good man and we like you, but this particular job is not suited for you.

"I am going to recommend that you tell the others that you are leaving. I have the feeling that sales work would be good for you and suggest that you look around for a sales job. I will give you some time off to do that. I will see that your pay is ready for you in two weeks, and I hope we can make this change with as little friction as possible."

John Simpson said, "I'm sorry that you feel this way. I did like it here and I wanted to make a go of it. However, maybe you are right. I must admit that during the last month I have not been too happy with the tremendous amount of detail on the job. I do like working with people. Maybe I would like sales work better. I will look elsewhere for a job of this type."

John Simpson is not likely to be happy with this situation because nobody likes to feel that the initiative in a change of job came from the boss and that they had to go. Eventually he may be very pleased that he has made the change. In a sales job, he may find the area for which he is most suited and he may come back to Bill Watson some day to thank him for suggesting that he make this change.

Bill Watson will feel he has done the right thing to get this man out of a job where he was having a disrupting effect on the staff and where he had a tendency to be careless with detail. Other people on the staff are likely to breath a sigh of relief that Simpson has gone, because he was causing some of them to work overtime and he was lowering the productivity of the department.

14

CONCLUSION

Your job as a manager is to confine yourself to those activities which you alone can do because of your position and authority. Everything else you should delegate. This sounds like an easy job, but it isn't. Because as a manager you can't get rid of responsibility by giving it to others. You still must take full responsibility. That's what makes your job tough.

From time to time, of course, every manager or supervisor has to do certain technical work in his department. For example, the sales manager may occasionally do some selling. The office manager may at times assist in the preparation of financial statements or the completion of a trial balance. The production manager may at times do certain technical jobs in the plant. These special duties are part of the jobs of these managers.

However, while they are doing this technical work, they are not managing. The unfortunate thing is that while they are occupied with technical work, nobody else is managing, because nobody else has the authority or know-how to do the planning, organizing, controlling, motivating, and developing of people which are the basic duties of the manager.

The less technical and routine work the manager does and the more he concentrates on developing other people to do this work, the better job he will do as a manager.

Managing sounds easy, but actually it is one of the most difficult jobs for these reasons: People are difficult. They have their complexes and varying attitudes, their variety of experiences, training, and knowledge which makes them complicated and hard to understand.

It is difficult to change men. Yet we all change a little every time we have a new experience, every time we read a book, every time we meet a new personality. Although men can't be changed in their deep-seated basic personality, temperament, and character qualities, it is possible to change them in other ways. As managers, this is what we are really attempting to do. We are trying to change men. We coach men, we counsel them, we try to communicate with them, we have annual performance reviews with them, we reprimand them, and in all these things we are attempting to change them.

If it were possible to change men radically, to change their temperament, personality, and character, motivating men would be a very easy job. All you would have to do would be to change men and make them into hard workers. You'd take the sloppy ones and make them thorough. You'd take the people who can't get along with others on your staff and make them into perfect workers. Then your job would be very simple because you'd get perfect work from everyone. But you've tried to do this and it doesn't work—you've tried to change people and you find that you can't really change them.

That's why selection of personnel is one of the most important jobs in management. If you hire good men, you don't have to change them. If you hire weak men, you can't change them very much and you are left trying to do a job with a weak crew. Management and supervision are not the achievement of things, but the development and motivation of people who can achieve things. Only when we learn how to develop and motivate people can we become good mana gers. The easy way to manage, of course, would be to change men, so let's take a look and see in what ways we can change them.

First of all, we can change a man's attitudes. It's difficult, but sometimes a man's attitudes can be changed. For example, suppose you have a man on your staff who is a Communist and his attitudes are such that he hates free enterprise and thinks that people who work for a capitalistic organization are suckers. He thinks that business is a racket and business organizations exploit the unsuspecting worker. His attitude toward you and your company is to take you for everything he can get. He will try to do as little as he can, take all the advantages he can get, and do everything he can to jeopardize your efficiency because he feels that the more he can undermine this racket, the sooner his ideal world will come into being.

After he has worked with you for a while and he sees that you are treating him fairly, that you pay him what he's worth for the job he does, that you go out of your way to try to help him and develop him, that you are willing to go beyond the call of duty and take an interest in him as a person, and that you live up to your promises, his attitudes change a little and now he says to himself, "This isn't a bad guy I'm working for. Maybe I should go to work for him a little," and so he becomes more cooperative. Then when he sees that your company policy is fair and that management is not trying to exploit him, but is rather trying to help him and is trying to make a cooperative effort out of production and efficiency, his attitude toward your management may change.

In time, as he works with you and sees the way you operate, his attitudes may change to the degree that he may even drop his Communistic thinking and become a believer in private enterprise. He may start to believe in the opportunities the free-enterprise system gives a man to show his initiative and develop himself on the basis of his capabilities.

You have changed this man's attitudes by the manner in which you treated him. If you are a good leader and if you are good at motivating men, eventually you will be able to improve the attitudes of all the people who work for you.

Another thing you are constantly trying to change about men is their knowledge. The more knowledge you give a person, the better understanding he has. This is why education is so important. The more knowledge he has, the quicker he catches on and the more perceptive he is. The manager's job is to try to give people more knowledge of the job. You do this by training them and again by counseling and coaching and trying to develop them.

Sometimes you give them training courses within the company and at other times you send them outside for training. You also impart knowledge to people about the job, company policy, company products, and about what you are trying to achieve. The better your ability to communicate, the more knowledge you give men. Your job is a constant struggle to increase the knowledge of your people.

Another thing that can be changed in men is their skills. Men can improve their skills. You help them do this of course by training. Sometimes you go beyond improving their technical skills and try to improve their skills in communicating through courses in public speaking and human relations and by coaching and counseling. Every manager should be constantly trying to increase the skills of his men. The more skillful his people get, the more effective they will be in achieving his goals.

One other thing you can change about men is their experience. Men come to you with specific experiences, but when you get them on your staff, you can give them new experiences. This is what you do when you shift a man from one job to another. You give him wider experience, and the wider experience he has, the better he usually does any job. The greater his experience in business, the more useful he will be in any particular field.

The ultimate aim is that all decisions will be made as you as a manager or the head of the department would make them. You make decisions better than men in specialized jobs in your department because you have greater over-all knowledge. The more you can help the men in your department to acquire this over-all knowledge, the better their decision-making will become.

It's wise policy to switch men around in their jobs to help them gain more experience. Occasionally you may ask them to do a part of your job or you may let them try their wings by doing your entire job for a day with you coaching from the side lines. This motivates them and it's a way of commending them. It's a way of showing you have confidence in them; it's a way of giving recognition, and it stimulates men and gives them an opportunity to try out a different set of skills.

The manager's job or the supervisor's job is not the achievement of things but the development of people who achieve things. The way he develops people is by trying to change them. He tries to change their attitudes, their knowledge, their skills, and their experiences. He tries to do this through all the techniques at his command which have been described in this book.

In everything he does the manager is constantly trying to motivate men. He does this by trying to satisfy the needs of men. He shows them how if they work and perform efficiently, they will gain satisfaction, make more money, and get more recognition. They will have opportunity to get ahead. They will feel that they belong to the group, they will be treated with respect, and their dignity as workers will be maintained.

The good manager is constantly trying to motivate men by studying them as individuals. He soon finds that every man is exactly like every other man in that he has certain needs that he must satisfy, but each man is completely different than every other man in that he has a different combination of needs.

For example, recognition may be very important to one man but unimportant to another. One man will respond to praise, and to another man, praise doesn't mean a thing. One man may want opportunity because he is really ambitious. To another man, security is the most important thing. It is very important to another man that he be liked and accepted and belong and be part of the team.

The good manager learns that he must work with men generally on the basis of their need satisfaction and he must work with specific men on the basis of their specific needs.

A successful manager is not going to be a weak leader. He is going to be strong and demanding, and he will not let people push him around. He knows that he will not gain the confidence or admiration of his men by being easy. Men respect a boss who is strong and knows what he wants, but who will treat them fair, stand behind them, and live up to his promises. A boss who will let them know where they stand and who is competent, knows his business, and can lead them to success. They will follow him because they are anxious to be on a winning team.

This doesn't mean that good human relations aren't important. A good manager or a good supervisor can be firm and demanding, but he can still practice good human relations. He must show respect for the men on his staff. He must have confidence in them.

On the other hand, if a manager is lacking in technical

competence and sincerity, no matter how smooth he is in human relations, he will fail to gain the confidence of his staff. Men are quick to detect insincerity or lack of knowledge, and they will soon lose faith in such a manager.

When you come to analyze his job, the manager is really working for his men. His job is to coach men and teach them and develop them. His job is to work for them, to bring them the best in training and guidance and leadership. In return, the men do the job.

As long as they are treated fairly and with understanding and have faith in the competence of his leadership, they will follow him and do what he asks. The ultimate result will be well motivated people and a very successful operation.